WALKING MIRACLE

WALKING MIRACLE

HOW FAITH, POSITIVE THINKING, AND PASSION FOR FOOTBALL BROUGHT ME BACK FROM PARALYSIS... AND HELPED ME FIND PURPOSE

RYAN SHAZIER
WITH LARRY PLATT

GRAND CENTRAL
PUBLISHING

NEW YORK   BOSTON

Grand Central Publishing
Hachette Book Group
1290 Avenue of the Americas, New York, NY 10104
grandcentralpublishing.com
twitter.com/grandcentralpub

First Edition: November 2021

Grand Central Publishing is a division of Hachette Book Group, Inc. The Grand Central Publishing name and logo is a trademark of Hachette Book Group, Inc.

The publisher is not responsible for websites (or their content) that are not owned by the publisher.

The Hachette Speakers Bureau provides a wide range of authors for speaking events. To find out more, go to www.hachettespeakersbureau.com or call (866) 376-6591.

Library of Congress Cataloging-in-Publication Data
Names: Shazier, Ryan, author. | Platt, Larry, author.
Title: Walking miracle: how faith, positive thinking, and passion for football brought me back from paralysis...and helped me find purpose / Ryan Shazier with Larry Platt.
Identifiers: LCCN 2021032992 | ISBN 9781538706251 (hardcover) | ISBN 9781538706275 (ebook)
Subjects: LCSH: Shazier, Ryan. | Pittsburgh Steelers (Football team)—History. | Football players—United States—Biography. | Football injuries—Patients—Rehabilitation—United States—Biography. | Paralytics—Rehabilitation—United States—Biography.
Classification: LCC GV939.S436 A3 2021 | DDC 796.33092 [B]—dc23
LC record available at https://lccn.loc.gov/2021032992

ISBNs: 978-1-5387-0625-1 (hardcover), 978-1-5387-0627-5 (ebook), 978-1-5387-0787-6 (BN.com signed edition)

Printed in the United States of America

LSC-C

Printing 1, 2021

For Michelle, my love;
R.J. and Lyon, my motivation;
and my parents, for showing me the way.

He is a wise man who does not grieve for the things which he has not, but rejoices for those which he has.

—*Epictetus*

CONTENTS

CONTENTS

WALKING MIRACLE

INTRODUCTION
"YA GOTTA *SHALIEVE*!"

Man, Ryan, you're not okay. That's what I said to myself about two weeks in. I'd developed a urinary tract infection, and I had a fever. Even though the doctors had told me all about the spinal cord injury I'd suffered, even though they'd told me I only had a 20 percent chance of ever walking again, until now I'd assumed that I was going to get better.

When it first happened, when a routine tackle against the Bengals on the turf of Cincinnati's Paul Brown Stadium left me with a burning sensation in my lower back and no feeling in my legs, my first thought had been, *It's a stinger*—a nerve injury common in football that can temporarily send tingling, numbness, or loss of feeling, usually down the arm. *No big deal.* After the chopper ride from Cincinnati to Pittsburgh and surgery days later, I still had faith. I'd grown up in football and the church; I'd grown up following game plans. My new game plan was to figure out what I had to do in order to get better.

My faith had always been my not-so-secret weapon. When I was growing up in Fort Lauderdale, Florida, my dad, Vernon Shazier, was a preacher and my mom, Shawn, was a God-fearing, walking advertisement for the Golden Rule. They're humble, loving, everyday folks. From them, I learned that God always has a plan for me. Mom used to tell me, "Whenever you're in a tough situation, find a light in it." In every situation, there's always a way to focus on the good in it and not the bad—it's just a matter of attitude. When I was five, my hair started falling out. I mean, in clumps. I was diagnosed with alopecia areata, an autoimmune disease that causes patchy hair loss. Imagine going to kindergarten bald. Kids can be less than tactful, and sometimes they're downright mean. Mom's take on it? "Ryan, God *chose* you to be bald," she said.

Who was I to question His plan? It had been drummed into me: faith would set me free. But now, just two weeks after the play that would change my life, my faith was starting to crack.

Man, Ryan, you're not okay, I kept telling myself. My cousin Nehari Crawford, who played football at Duquesne University, was seated by my hospital bed. Nehari had always looked up to me; I'd been his mentor. Now he was seeing me paralyzed from the waist down, feverish, sick to my stomach. I'd always been strong; *strength*, man, that was my *thing*. Now I was anything but. I felt the sickness rising in me and turned my head to throw up, but the vomit hit the rail on the side of my bed and some of it ricocheted back at me. *You're not okay, Ryan.*

That's when it started, the rush of "why me" thoughts. I'd always done the right thing: worked hard, treated people with respect and kindness. I'd been raised to believe that if you follow the rules, good things will happen. You get back what you put out there. And now…*this*? Fourteen days ago, I'd been a world-class athlete; now here I was, vomit-covered, feverish, unable to take a step or raise a leg or feel anything below the waist.

Why, God?

Why me?

What did I do to deserve this?

* * *

In the years since my injury, you may have caught glimpses of me in a string of viral, feel-good moments. There I was, limping—but *walking*—onto the stage at the 2018 NFL Draft to loud applause before a packed, emotional auditorium. There I was, dancing at my wedding just seventeen months after the play that had left me paralyzed. Or you may have seen my return to Heinz Field on a football Sunday, waving the Terrible Towel to the cheering Steelers faithful from my wheelchair. Or you may have seen the giant "Get Well Soon, Ryan!" card in downtown Pittsburgh signed by fans from all over the world.

But those viral moments since December 4, 2017, don't really tell the full story of these last four years. Because it hasn't been all inspiration and smiles. *Walking Miracle* is the story of a comeback attempt—a comeback from paralysis, yes, but also a comeback from doubt. It's also more than that. It's really a story about the power of faith *and* the questioning of that faith; about the role positive thinking can play in healing; about the lessons for overcoming adversity found in a brutal game; about love, between a man and woman—I don't know where I'd be without my wife, Michelle—but also love between a city and an athlete, and how, in a crazy way, one always seemed to inspire the other.

I'd always stared down odds. How many kids get alopecia at five years old? How many refuse to let it define them? How many kids are told in high school that they'll never be able to play the game they love again because of a severe case of scoliosis? How many are able to play anyway, and not only play but *dominate* at every level? How many kids play Division I football, let alone go on to the NFL and rise to Pro Bowl heights?

Long odds? *Don't bring that talk here*, I'd always thought. But you want a challenge? How about an

80 percent chance of living the rest of your life in a wheelchair?

This book is about what happens when things look so bleak you want to quit. How do you push through? It's about how you go from doubt to realizing, *Hey, maybe this is God's plan. Maybe I'm going through just what I'm meant to go through. Maybe, more than any tackle or interception on the field, overcoming paralysis is what I've been put here to do, to inspire others.* And it's about changing your thinking so that you see the opportunity that lurks in tragedy. I was twenty-five years old, and I'd thought of myself as a football player for nearly my whole life. Wreaking havoc on the football field was not only what I did; it was also how I saw myself. Coming face-to-face with the possibility that I'd have to rethink how I self-identified was more of a challenge than lining up against the meanest, biggest SOBs on any given Sunday.

How you get there, though, how you shift your thinking and embrace the obstacle as the way to growth—*that's* a little more complicated than the posting of a fun moment on Instagram might suggest.

That day in the hospital, when I vomited on myself? It unlocked a period of doubt and despair. Some moments, I'd feel depressed. *You're never getting better,* I'd think. Other times, I'd feel anger...at *Him. My dad served You his whole life; he tended to Your flock faithfully. How could You do this to him?*

But that day, in my fevered state, a hazy, fragmented

memory started to come to me. It was from a lighter, more carefree time, a day during the 2016 season, the year before my injury. We were all in my Porsche Panamera: me; my best friend and trainer, Jerome Howard; my then girlfriend, Michelle; and my little brother, Vernon II. I was talking about how, even though I was going to the Pro Bowl, I still had a chip on my shoulder.

"I just want to make everybody believe in Shazier, man," I said. "This is the year. The year everybody's gonna believe in me."

I was doing what great athletes do: they set goals and they tell themselves a story that helps them achieve them. My story was that no one believed in Shazier. I was going to make them believe.

"Believe in Shazier, I like that," Michelle said.

"*Shalieve!*" Jerome barked out. "You gonna make them *Shalieve!*"

My eyes lit up. That was it—*Ya gotta Shalieve!* Something about the phrase struck me. I'd always believed in myself. But I also thought it was something for my teammates and the fans: I wanted them to believe that, on the field, I'd be their truest fighter. For the rest of the ride, we were calling it out. Every time we saw a passerby outside our window: *"There's a Shaliever!"* We were laughing and high-fiving, energized by this fantasy of a city full of Shalievers.

Now, prone in a hospital bed, sick to my stomach, feverish, it came back to me, that image of all of us laughing, drunk on the power of belief. Through the haze, I knew. This wasn't just some fever-induced memory. No, this was a sign. This was God telling me He had a purpose for me that I might not understand.

Could it be just a coincidence that at the very moment my faith was starting to fail me, a flashback to pure positivity jumped to mind? Was this God's way of telling me what I needed right now? It was as if He was reminding me that though the stakes were higher than ever before, the prescription was the same. I needed to *Shalieve*, just like always.

CHAPTER ONE

"DADDY, PRAY FOR ME"

By the time I became an NFL All-Pro, I was like an addict, living for the adrenaline rush of making a big play on the field. I don't mean to make light of *real* addiction, mind you. But I really was hooked on the feeling that would shoot through me after forcing a running back to cough up the football or cutting off a passing lane and picking off a pass. You make the play and look at your opponents, and you can see how what you just did deflated them. They walk back to their huddle slumped over, their steps just a little more tentative than before. You've taken all their momentum and joy and given it to your team.

It wasn't just the forcing of turnovers. Ever since I was five years old, I'd lived for the big hit, the kind that's heard throughout the stadium, the kind that forces a collective gasp from the stands. You feel that *thwack* of body on body and then you stand over your opponent and you can almost see the self-confidence leave his body. You watch him gingerly get up (you always want him to get up) and you see him groggy or tentative or stumbling. You've stolen his swagger.

Football is such a fast game; to the untrained eye, it might appear that those big, thunderous tackles happen by accident. And while it's true that much of what happens on the field is pure reaction, the product of hours of repetitive practice meant to train muscle memory, it's also true that any tackle is about basic physics. In high school, my physics teacher never mentioned football, but what I *heard* was all about the game: the total force on a ball carrier is equal to the rate of change of momentum, and that momentum is the product of mass and velocity.

See, my dad, in addition to being a pastor, had been a high school defensive coach when I was in grade school. And he'd effectively been *my* unofficial coach since he'd held up a piece of paper in front of me when I was eight years old.

"Listen, Ryan, let's say this piece of paper is the ball carrier," he said, holding his other hand six inches behind the paper. "You actually don't want to tackle this piece of paper. You want to tackle this hand *behind* the paper. You want to tackle *through* the paper. Because it's easier to tackle somebody if you're tackling *through* them. Remember, they're trying to move forward, too."

9

It was my first lesson in the physics of football. My job wasn't to tackle the man in front of me; it was to tackle something *behind* him. And that led to physics lesson number two: doing that successfully was really all about momentum, and I had to use my speed to accelerate *into* the tackle, so the force was dictated by my side of the collision.

By the time I made it to the pros, before the NFL made helmet-to-helmet contact a penalty, I had a reputation for tackling with my head down, for leading with my helmet. Mind you, it's not that I was seen as a dirty player. It's just that I was always so focused on acceleration—on tackling through that paper—that I'd get there so fast and by the time I'd try to pick my head up, it was too late. I was already *there*.

We were all aware of this, my coaches and I. Even though helmet-to-helmet collisions weren't illegal yet, they were always dangerous. That's because of the biomechanics of the neck, which has a natural curve to it that allows it to act like a spring and absorb and disperse force. When a tackler drops his helmet and hits the ball carrier headfirst, he's not only increasing his own chances of suffering a concussion but also exposing his neck to breaking. That's because the impact sends a compressive force through the neck, causing it to become compacted and less able to absorb and dissipate the force of the hit.

I was very familiar with the stories about the dangers of headfirst tackling. Our defensive coordinator in Pittsburgh, Keith Butler, warned me about guys he had played with who had tackled with their heads down and had gotten injured. After every game, we'd watch the film of my tackles and freeze the video on the plays where my head was down. Before every practice, I'd attack a tackling dummy over and over again, concentrating on keeping my head up.

My trainer and best friend, Jerome, talked about it all the time. He'd played linebacker in high school and was on the All-America team in college. "Keep your head up, man!" he'd remind me, time and again.

And that's what was so funny—and by "funny," I mean "ironic"—about that routine play in Cincinnati on *Monday Night Football* on December 4, 2017. I'd managed to keep my head up; wouldn't you know it, *that's* when I got hurt.

I'd already made two tackles on the Bengals' opening possession, and I felt like I was flying across the field, which was funny—again, *ironic*—because I'd had a high ankle sprain and had been questionable for the game.

"Maybe you shouldn't play," Michelle had said. But when the doctors left it up to me at game time, did they really think I wouldn't give it a go for my teammates? Besides, we were in a race for home field advantage in the first round of the playoffs. With eighty-seven tackles and three interceptions in just eleven games, I was the leader of a defense that was fourth in the league, giving up 17.5 points per game. If I was walking, I was playing.

So there I was, bearing down on wide receiver Josh Malone, who'd just caught a checkdown pass from quarterback Andy Dalton. It was such a routine play that I had all kinds of time to read what was in front of me. So much time that, for the first time in my career, during a game I actually said to myself:

Keep your head up.

Just as I made contact with Malone, he turned, and that upturned head of mine made contact with his left hip. The next thing I knew, I was down. I instantly felt a sharp burning sensation in my lower back. I rolled over, clutching at my back. But while I could move my arms, I couldn't move my legs. I couldn't wiggle my toes. There was no feeling below the waist. My teammates gathered around. "I can't feel my legs," I said.

The once-deafening stadium had grown eerily silent. I lay there, hearing nothing but my own breath and the pounding of my heart. I could see our trainer moving my leg and asking if I could feel it. *Feel what?* I thought. Once in a while, a teammate would shout words of support. But as I was placed on a stretcher, I caught a glimpse of my teammates, many of them kneeling, their helmets off. Their facial expressions spoke volumes. I could see my man, linebacker Vince Williams, crying. Later, I'd read about the immediate fallout my injury had on my guys.

"I don't think Vince stopped crying until after half-time, and that's one of the most gangster dudes on the team," safety Mike Mitchell said. "People had to grab him by the face mask and be like, 'Yo, you're the middle linebacker now. You can't be sniffling.'"

I'd been where my teammates stood now. Football can be a brutal sport, played by massive men who collide at dangerous speeds. Usually, somehow, we walk away from our collisions, head back to our huddles and our trash talk. But when that doesn't happen, when you walk away from the carnage of a crash but one of your brothers on the field—on your team *or* the opposing team—doesn't get up and has to be carried off, you feel for him, yes, but you also feel the real-life terror of what we do, a terror we keep hidden away save for those moments. Now, as the ovation from the fans got fainter and fainter as I was wheeled down a tunnel and toward a waiting ambulance, I was face-to-face with that terror.

* * *

Stingers are an occupational hazard on the football field. They almost always occur after a tackle, usually when your shoulder is forced one way and your head and neck go the other. The result is a stretching of the brachial plexus, a nerve bundle that goes from the neck to the shoulder and down the arm. The nerves are temporarily stunned; as they try to recover, you're likely to feel a burning, stinging, or tingling sensation—along with a dead arm that just won't move.

You can watch that play in Cincinnati online now and see me roll over, clutching at my low back, where the burning was. You can also see me flexing my arms—checking to see if I had a dead arm. Nope.

Still, I was convinced this was just a stinger. That's the positive thinker in me. Mom didn't just tell me to "find a light" in every bad situation; she lived her life that way. As long as I could remember, she suffered from Crohn's disease. And I mean *suffered*. One year when I was growing up, she spent the holidays in the hospital. We celebrated Christmas with her there. We opened presents in her hospital room, and she never let us see how much agony she was in.

She'd have these flare-ups of inflammation in her digestive tract, which brought on terrible stomach pains, severe diarrhea, bone-crushing fatigue, and weight loss. But you'd never know from Mom that she was suffering. I remember visiting her in the hospital, and she was always smiling, always telling us stories about the lives of her nurses: this one was from Cuba, that one was paying off her crushing college debt. Both Mom and Dad were always positive-minded, but Mom, without preaching, always reminded my brother, Vernon II, and me that someone else had it worse and we should be grateful for what we had.

Mom had instilled in us a way of looking at the world. You didn't assume the worst, either of anyone else or of any situation you found yourself in. So as I lay on that stretcher in the tunnel of Paul Brown Stadium, it was only natural that I talked myself into believing that I'd only suffered a stinger. The feeling in my legs *would* come back.

In the tunnel, I called Michelle, my fiancée at the time. She hadn't yet turned on the game, but she was already receiving texts from friends with messages like "Hope he's okay" and "Praying for your family." By the time I reached her, she knew this was serious. She was crying, and it was up to me to comfort her. "Michelle, calm down," I said. "We're going to get through this." I'd probably end up missing a couple of weeks, I told her.

My next call was to my dad. "Daddy, pray for me," I said. "I can't feel my legs."

"Son, we're going to be all right," he said, though I could hear the fear in his voice. Ever since high school, Dad and I would pray together before my games. In the NFL, I had many teammates who would prepare for a game by pounding each other on the shoulder pads while screaming or by blaring heavy metal or rap music. Hey, whatever works. I'd prepare by praying with my dad. We'd never pray for a win or a big play. We'd pray for my health and well-being, and for the health and well-being of everyone on the field that day. We'd pray for those we loved and those we hardly knew.

Dad suggested that we do that now. "Lord, please

watch over Ryan and let his body heal," Dad said, his voice thick with emotion. "We trust in you, Lord, and that You have a message, and that You'll lead us to Your message."

I could tell that both Michelle and Dad were scared and upset, but they were strong for me. In fact, I learned later that both cried many times over the following months, amid all of the lows and highs, all of the stress. But neither ever let me see them cry. Dad later said he'd cry fifteen or twenty times a day. But I didn't know that at the time. Growing up, he was our family's patriarch, and he was dead set against letting me see any doubt or weakness.

After my injury, I'd get a text from Dad every day: *"God is with you. God is helping you. God is healing you."* He'd send a different text to Mom, Vernon II, and Michelle every day, too, coaching them through the stress and trauma of what we were all dealing with— even while he himself struggled.

Mike Tyson once said, "Everyone has a plan until they get punched in the mouth." As a man of faith, Dad knew how easy it was to have one's faith tested in times of crisis. "I needed for the family to know that we were not alone, God had not abandoned us," he told me later. "God had not moved. He was still sustaining us, as He had done for all those years."

Mom also put on a brave face. I learned later that she would guard my hospital door; whenever a visitor approached, she'd make clear to them in no uncertain terms that there was to be no crying once they entered my room. "Let it out now," she'd tell them. I got nothing but positivity from the people who loved me, which in turn made *me* more positive.

The Steelers had two world-class neurosurgeons from the University of Pittsburgh Medical Center (UPMC) on staff, Dr. David Okonkwo and Dr. Joseph Maroon. Dr. Okonkwo—"Dr. O"—traveled to maybe one away game a year, and the game in Cincinnati was the one that year. From the moment I lay on that turf, Dr. O rarely left my side. He was with us in Cincinnati because Dr. Maroon was in—if you can believe it—Kazakhstan, making a house call: the prime minister was having back pain. "I think God put me in Kazakhstan so you could be there for Ryan," Dr. Maroon later said to Dr. O.

Dr. O has a youthful way about him, but make no mistake: he's a badass doc who has lectured around the globe on the treatment of traumatic injuries to the brain and spine. In the ambulance on the way to the University of Cincinnati Medical Center, he asked me to wiggle my toes.

Lo and behold, there it was—a wiggle. Fifteen minutes ago, on the field, I hadn't even been able to do that. "That's a good sign," Dr. O said. Of course, I started asking the doc questions about when I could play again. "Think I'll be ready to go by the Houston game?" I asked.

"Let's not get ahead of ourselves," Dr. O said,

patting my arm. He later said that, starting in that ambulance, I'd ask him *every day* when I could play again. In the months to come, I would learn just how Dr. O approached his calling: one part medical provider, one part psychologist, one part friend.

With Dr. O at my side, I was rushed into the trauma unit at the University of Cincinnati Medical Center. There, I was suddenly surrounded by a sea of doctors in white coats and concerned-looking nurses, all looking down at me. I couldn't even see the wall behind them; all I could see were all these health-care professionals, poking and prodding me.

I remember thinking that all these doctors and nurses must have been wondering who Dr. O was, given that he was dressed in a Steelers sweatshirt and a Steelers baseball cap. *Is he a coach?* Just when I thought someone was going to ask him to leave, bursting through the door came Dr. Joseph Cheng, the hospital's chair of neurological surgery. He put his hand on Dr. O's shoulder and addressed the roomful of docs and nurses.

"None of you know who this guy is," Dr. Cheng said, "but if we just do what he says, everything is going to go much easier for all of us."

Bam—now my guy was in charge. "We are going to be judged by a million subject-matter idiots," Dr. O told Dr. Cheng and his staff. "What we do here will be scrutinized forever, so we're going to get this right and we're going to try everything."

I've spent my life in locker rooms and have sat through more motivational speeches than I can remember. Dr. O's comments in that room put everyone on the same mission, together. *That's* great leadership.

Ever the optimist, I was still holding out hope that I'd suffered a stinger, but Dr. O knew that wasn't the case. When he first knelt down next to me on that field, he knew this was a catastrophic injury, he later told me. A stinger is basically weakness in a muscle group that gradually fades as strength returns. But I had no feeling in my legs. I had a complete loss of function, and Dr. O knew the statistics in that case: a *3 percent* chance of ever walking again.

Rather than tell me that, Dr. O just calmly ordered a series of MRIs and CT scans. Later, I came to understand that he didn't believe in talking to patients in percentages because the percentages refer to populations, not individuals, which totally squares with my way of looking at things. It may have been a fact that only 3 percent of those who lose total function in their legs ever walk again, but that didn't mean those are *my* odds, right? After all, as the night wore on, I was becoming a master at wiggling my toes—which meant, I later learned, that I was looking at something more like a 20 percent of walking again. I was getting better already, right?

* * *

Dad was at church when the first call came from the Steelers telling him I'd been hurt. Then, as he was racing home, his phone rang again. "This is serious," the team representative told him. "You and Mrs. Shazier need to get here."

The Steelers flew Michelle in from Pittsburgh and Mom, Dad, and Vernon II from Florida. Mom liked to say there was *always* something to find hope in, even in the worst situation—if only you looked hard enough. Well, when they landed on the private runway at the Cincinnati airport, a complete stranger overheard Dad say to Mom, "We need to get transportation to the hospital."

"Excuse me," he said to Dad. "Are you Mr. Shazier?"

He was a businessman about to depart for Florida on a private plane. He was also a former Bengal—lineman Alex Sulfsted, who, after his playing days, had built a successful career in real estate. He'd watched the game and seen my injury, and had actually been trying to reach our quarterback, Ben Roethlisberger, who he knew, to see if he could help in any way. Now he recognized my parents at the airport.

"I won't be here for a few days," he told my dad, extending a hand holding his car keys. "Take my truck."

"Take your what?" Dad said, not sure he'd heard right. But he had. And Sulfsted was insistent. They exchanged cell phone numbers, and Mom, Dad, and Vernon II rode off in Alex Sulfsted's Range Rover.

Can you imagine that? A complete stranger, handing over the keys to his car?

There are angels everywhere, if only you're open to them.

Mom, Dad, and Michelle arrived at the hospital to good news. On early Tuesday morning, the morning after the injury, Dr. O explained that my body was waking up. Not only was I wiggling my toes, but I was able to move my thigh ever so slightly.

But the hopefulness that news inspired was short-lived. By Wednesday morning, I could no longer wiggle my toes. I'd slid back to the same state I had been in on the field: No feeling in my legs. A total lack of function.

An MRI showed I'd developed a blood clot, which was putting pressure on my spine.

This was going to be more complicated.

In effect, my injury had stimulated an inflammatory response, prompting the clotting. Remember Dr. O's promise to "try everything"? Well, he attacked that blood clot like a pass rusher. He shot me full of a high dose of steroids, attacking the inflammation. And he drove my blood pressure up to raise my oxygen levels and send healthy cells into the spinal cord. Then came the torture of hypothermia.

"There's reason to believe that, if we cool the injury, it will give it a better chance of recovering," Dr. O explained. He stressed that this wouldn't be pleasant.

I was all in. "Let's go for it," I said.

They wrapped me for hours in what was, in effect, an ice machine. The thirty-three-degree cold acted like an analgesic, calming the inflammation and reducing the swelling. I had to try to sleep through the night while shivering—all the self-coaching in the world couldn't remove me from *that* reality.

The decision was made that I'd head back to Pittsburgh for surgery that would be performed by Dr. O and Dr. Maroon. But time was of the essence. The clot seemed to be breaking up, but I wasn't out of the woods yet. I had to get to Pittsburgh quickly, so I was airlifted to UPMC on an air ambulance.

I'm not going to lie. It sure is easy to start asking yourself "*Why me?*" at times like this. But as I was lying there, my legs tightly wrapped in compression stockings to prevent any new clots from developing, whenever those "*woe is me*" thoughts started to bubble up, I would turn my attention to thoughts of that businessman and former player, Alex Sulfsted, whose car Mom and Dad was using.

He'd even gone a step further and insisted on flying them and Michelle to Pittsburgh on his private plane. It was smaller than the private jet the team had chartered for them, so Mom was a bit nervous— she doesn't love to fly. But I couldn't help but break into a smile when I thought of Michelle and my folks in that dude's plane. His generosity and compassion made me feel hopeful and grateful. *How lucky am I? I* thought to myself, which sounds kind of crazy given my circumstance, I know.

And when I *did* fall back into disbelief, when I did wonder to myself, *How is this happening? How'd I get here?* I decided to take the question literally. Partly to take my mind off of what I was facing, I started thinking back. It wasn't like my life was flashing before my eyes or anything like that. It was more that, lying in that air ambulance, it was comforting and calming to think back to when I'd met my first love and fallen hard for the game of football.

CHAPTER TWO

FAITH. DISCIPLINE. INTEGRITY.

When I was five years old, my parents introduced me to a bunch of different sports to see what I'd like. I was too fast-paced for basketball—too aggressive, always committing fouls. Baseball? I had no hand-eye coordination. Track? That was way too much running if you weren't chasing after somebody holding a ball.

Football, though? Love at first sight. Even then—at five years old!—I liked hitting rather than being hit. My parents knew it, too, and my dad was not uninterested in my passion for football. In fact, he fueled it. Growing up in Fort Pierce, Florida, he'd been quite the player himself. But when his mother went through a very bad divorce—she took her four kids and fled a domestic abuse situation—he found himself living in Fort Lauderdale's projects. In high school, he gave up football in order to work and help his mother put food on the table. Everything he did was oriented toward lessening his mother's burden, including his enlistment in the navy after high school. He knew he'd get a paycheck he could send home, three squares a day, and the discipline he'd need throughout life.

Dad always felt he had been robbed of his own football dream, and he was determined to make sure nothing would interfere with mine. He was the defensive coordinator at Blanche Ely High School, and there I was, even at five years old, by his side at every practice and game.

You could say that Dad lived vicariously through me on the football field, but he wasn't overbearing about it. When my little brother, Vernon II, played, he didn't exhibit the same drive that I did. He was a good player—six foot three and quick; Dad used to say he could be another Richard Sherman. But although Vernon liked playing on game day, he didn't seem very committed, and that was fine with Dad.

For me, though, football was everything. Growing up, if I wasn't in church, odds were that I was on a football field with my friends. Mom and Dad let me play in a pee wee football league in a rougher part of town, Lauderdale Lakes. Those kids came from tougher backgrounds and were more advanced than me on the field. That helped me grow; soon, I was putting them down.

When I was in middle school, Dad had the calling to follow the Lord. With hardly anything in the bank, he packed us up and moved us to Waco, Texas, so he could attend seminary. From there, he still coached Blanche High's defense remotely, watching practices on the computer. When Blanche High played for the state championship, the school flew him in.

In the meantime, I started playing in a Texas pee wee football league with the kids of a bunch of good ole boys. One day, the director of the league pulled Dad aside. "Some of the parents are complaining that Ryan tackles a little too hard," he said.

"What do you want me to do?" Dad asked. "Tell him not to be so rough? This is *football*."

Dad had a plan for me. He was building a linebacker. He'd pop a tape of Lawrence Taylor into the VCR and tell me to watch closely. "You've gotta be a high-motor, relentless guy," he'd say. "The kind of guy who puts terror into anyone lined up against him. The kind of guy who tells the opposing tackle or tight end, 'You better not take one play off, or your quarterback is paying a visit to them paramedics over there.'"

Dad used to say he was "building a cheetah": you can't escape a cheetah. That required working on my mental *and* physical stamina. He'd have me run twenty-yard sprints—hundreds of them—with thirty seconds in between. The purpose wasn't the running; it was the time between sprints. He was training that high motor to recover in time for the next play.

After about three years, we moved back to Fort Lauderdale, where Dad became assistant pastor at Mount Bethel Baptist Church.

At first, I convinced Mom and Dad to let me go to Blanche Ely High, where Dad coached. They subscribed to the "let 'em test the waters, but don't let 'em drown" school of parenting, so they relented, even though Ely High had a reputation as a school with lots of disciplinary problems. After my JV football season my sophomore year, I got into two fights, and Mom and Dad had had enough. My dad's best friend, Steve Davis, had been Ely's offensive coordinator. But when he moved on to be the head coach at Plantation High, I went there, too.

At Plantation High, I flourished. Dad had been building a linebacker, but Coach Davis moved me to defensive end. I was about 180 pounds—there was no way I could play defensive lineman in college. But in South Florida high school football, I was either too fast for a lineman to block me or too strong for a running back to keep me from the quarterback. My junior season I had twenty-two sacks.

But Dad didn't just teach me about a game. He and Mom modeled resilience and forgiveness in their everyday lives. Mom, in how she smiled her way through Crohn's and treated everyone with dignity and respect. And Dad, in the way he'd turned his dysfunctional upbringing into a positive, impactful life.

His daddy was a longshoreman, and for a time

Dad and his siblings lived in a typical middle-class environment. But then his dad fell prey to alcohol and drugs, and the beatings started. His mom or the kids—it didn't matter who was on the receiving end of his father's abuse. His father would disappear for long stretches and then return, wreaking havoc and horror.

At one point in his teen years, Dad bought himself a .22-caliber pistol. "If he beats Mama today, I'm gonna kill him," Dad pledged to himself. That day, though they argued, his father didn't lay a hand on his mother. "Jesus was looking out for me that day," Dad says now.

Even after they escaped to the Fort Lauderdale projects, Dad hung on to his anger for decades. Then, after not hearing a thing from his father for damn near twenty-five years, he got word that his father was in the hospital. He'd had eight strokes.

What did Dad do? He and his siblings and his mom went to see this old, beaten-down man, who had no one in his life. And not only that: they took him in once he was discharged. For the next ten years, they were the caretaker to their former tormentor. My grandfather didn't speak much. But when Dad would ask if he was cold and place a blanket around his shoulders, the old man would break into tears, a frail shell of a man. "I think the fact that *we* would take him in blew him away," Dad says now. "He was so ashamed and guilty over what he'd done to us."

Dad's whole life, in other words, was a lesson in how to get through bad times and not let yourself be eaten up by bitterness. In his eulogy for my grandfather, Dad recalled a candy his father used to give to his kids. "He was bittersweet, just like that candy," he said.

That's who Dad is—he models what it means to be a man. He had a saying that, much to his displeasure, I had etched into my skin as a freshman in college: *Faith. Discipline. Integrity.* (Vernon II got the same tattoo when he was a senior in high school, leading Dad to joke that maybe he'd get it also. But he's too afraid of needles to ever really do it.)

When I was in high school, Dad became the part-time chaplain for the Miami Dolphins. One day, he asked me to go for a ride with him. "I want to talk to you," he said.

"In high school, and in life generally, you're gonna hear guys talk about three things: girls, money, and drugs," he said, slowly cruising our neighborhood. "A lot of kids are gonna say they get a lot of pussy— they don't. They'll say they got money, but they don't. And if they do, they probably schemed or scammed someone out of it. And drugs, well, you know that can put you in jail and jeopardize everything you're working for, son."

There was a pause. "If you want something in life, you need to sacrifice for it, son," he said. "Everyone *wants* to be successful—but the elephant in the room is sacrifice and its first cousin, discipline."

Every year, Dad would sit me down and have me write out my goals. Then he'd say: "Now, what behaviors and practices are you willing to commit to in order to achieve these goals?"

You might imagine that a teenager might roll his eyes at such an exercise. But Dad, who serves the folks in his congregation as one part spiritual mentor and one part life coach, explained why it mattered so much: "A dream without sacrifice and discipline is just vanity," he'd say. "It's just empty words."

Time and again, I got the message from my mom and dad that there would be rough times in the future. There's no such thing as smooth sailing. Turbulence is part of life. It's our job to navigate those rough waters, to remain calm in the storm, and to chart a course forward. That's what Mom did with Crohn's disease. It's a terrible disease, but you'd never hear that from her. She always found a light in her situation.

And me? I was no stranger to challenge. Heck, when I was born, I had over one hundred allergies. I was even allergic to baby formula. Then, when I was five years old and sported a thick baby 'fro, my hair started falling out. And not just on my head, either. My pillow would have a bunch of eyelashes on it every morning. My mom would run her hand through my 'fro and come out with a handful of curls.

The first few doctors couldn't tell us what was going on. My parents were worried to death. Finally, a dermatologist explained to my mom that my immune system was mistakenly attacking my hair follicles, forcing all the hair on my body to fall out. It was an autoimmune disease called alopecia areata.

Alopecia affects about 6.8 million people in the United States, causing hair loss on the scalp, face, and other parts of the body. It's a polygenic disease, meaning both parents must contribute a number of specific genes in order for their child to develop it. As a result, most parents with alopecia do not pass it on to their children. In fact, even among identical twins—who have the same genes—there's only a 55 percent chance that both will have it. That's why most doctors say it's more than a genetic disease, that environmental factors must also contribute to it.

Even before I was diagnosed with alopecia, I'd had many allergies. Could they have been related? No one knew for sure. Most doctors believe something— a virus, maybe, or something in the environment— triggers the reaction. But all I knew was that I looked way different from the other kids at school. Try explaining what alopecia is to children in the classroom or on the playground. Kids at that age can lack tact, right? So I had kids coming right up to me and asking if I had cancer. "Are you dying?" they'd ask.

No matter how many times I told them I had a disease that made my hair fall out, they'd still tease me. Let me tell you, kids can be downright mean. I heard it all: *Cue ball. Patches. Chia Pet.*

Sometimes I'd get angry. Sometimes I'd cry. I didn't even understand what was happening to my body, and other kids were treating me like I had the plague. At a time when most kids want to blend in, I was always different. Every day. Today, I meet kids (and some adults) with alopecia who struggle with self-esteem issues, and I tell them I get it. I've been where they're at.

When we moved from Fort Lauderdale to Waco, Texas, and again when we moved back to Florida three years later, I was the new kid in school. And the only thing meaner than a classmate in elementary school or middle school is a classmate who doesn't know you. So I heard it all. Twice.

If you read up on childhood teasing, you'll find that between 9 and 15 percent of those who are teased as kids suffer as adults with low self-esteem, anxiety, and even depression. But my parents, God bless 'em, showed me how to turn a negative into a positive. They didn't call those other kids' parents to get them to stop or yell at my teacher for not protecting me enough. That would've just made things worse. They told me I could decide to wear a hat, but that I'd have to wear it *all* the time. And a wig was out of the question. The alopecia wasn't going to go away. I couldn't hide from it, so I had to learn to live with it.

"There's nothing wrong with you," my mom would say. "You just don't have hair. Most kids do. That's it."

They made it *okay* for me to be different. And they told me that most teasers had themselves been teased. I pledged early on to not buy into that pattern. Everyone I met, I vowed, *I'd* treat with kindness and respect.

It was a familiar pattern: New school. New bald kid. New insults. And guess what? Florida kids aren't any different from Texas kids. *Magic 8 ball. Cancer boy. Professor X.* "If kids are teasing you about being different, it's because they're not feeling good about themselves," Mom said.

So I'd turn the tables. "For you to make fun of me, you probably got something going on with yourself," I'd say. "What don't you like about you?"

Or I'd tell them, "Crack jokes all you want. All you're doing is talking about my head. What else you got?" And then I'd laugh. 'Cause that's how you win against a bully. That's how you really piss them off. Laugh. Smile. Don't give a damn what they think.

Throughout high school, I tried countless treatments to stop my hair from falling out completely. One of them was a steroid cream I'd rub on my head and eyebrows. Unfortunately, with that stuff my hair only grew back in patches. I really *did* start to look like a Chia Pet.

Then there were the cortisone shots. They were supposed to stimulate hair growth by suppressing the immune system around my head and eyebrows. Again, I'd get a few patches of hair back on my head and eyebrows, but having thick needles jabbed into my skull thirty times every two weeks got pretty old pretty quick.

When I went to The Ohio State University, my mom asked if I wanted to keep getting the shots. That's when I decided to embrace baldness. My teammates at Ohio State didn't care. My coaches didn't care. I was bald when I was chasing my dreams, and I was bald when I was living 'em. So who really cared?

That's my message to people I meet today with alopecia who really struggle with it and won't go anywhere without a hat. I know how tough it is. But I tell them to look at it this way: If your hair magically grew back tomorrow, it wouldn't change who you are, or what you're capable of, or who loves you. I was the bald kid in high school. Then I was the bald kid at Ohio State. Then I was the bald guy in the NFL. And now I was the bald guy in a hospital room, fighting not only to walk but to maybe even play football again.

CHAPTER THREE

"NO ONE HAS EVER HAD THIS INJURY BEFORE"

If you're even a casual fan of football, you know that the sport has a history of spinal cord injuries and paralysis on the field. In the NFL, in the late seventies there was the tragedy of wide receiver Darryl Stingley, who, while lunging for a pass in a preseason game, jammed his helmet into a defensive back's shoulder pad. His fourth and fifth cervical vertebrae were compressed, rendering him paralyzed; Stingley spent the rest of his life as a quadriplegic.

More recently, there was the Buffalo Bills' Kevin Everett, who, in 2007, suffered a fracture and dislocation of the cervical spine—an injury first described as "life-threatening." Initially, Everett couldn't even move his eyes. Eventually, after months of intensive rehab, he walked again.

At the collegiate level, maybe the most well-known

case is that of Marc Buoniconti, the son of Hall of Fame linebacker Nick Buoniconti. Marc was a nineteen-year-old linebacker playing for The Citadel in 1985 when he was paralyzed from the shoulders down while making a tackle.

His father started the Miami Project to Cure Paralysis and the Buoniconti Fund at the University of Miami, which has become a cutting-edge investigative research program for spinal cord and brain injuries. Nick died at seventy-eight in 2019 after struggling with symptoms of chronic traumatic encephalopathy (CTE), a degenerative brain disease associated with repeated blows to the head. He was a great player, but it just may be that his most lasting legacy will be the work he did to raise money for research on spinal cord injuries.

Another well-known—and tragic—case is that of Chucky Mullins, a University of Mississippi defensive back who shattered his third, fourth, fifth, and sixth vertebrae while making a tackle in 1989. He never regained feeling below his neck.

But Mullins knew all about resilience. He'd been orphaned at a young age and had been seen as too small to play Division I football. But he'd defied the odds and made himself an integral part of the Ole Miss defense. His final tackle stopped a runner who outweighed him by fifty pounds at the goal line, preventing a touchdown.

Ole Miss raised over $1 million for the Chucky

Mullins Trust Fund. Chucky spent four months in the hospital and made good on his vow to return to school in a wheelchair and resume classes. However, a year later, he collapsed from a blood clot related to his injury and passed away.

More recently, there's been the inspirational story of Chris Norton, the college football player who suffered a spinal cord injury in 2010. Netflix recently aired *7 Yards: The Chris Norton Story*, which shows Chris's resilience after he was given only a 3 percent chance of ever walking again. After years of intense physical therapy, a 2015 video of Chris walking with the help of his then fiancée at his college graduation went viral, with more than 300 million views.

Those are just a few high-profile examples of the many spinal cord injuries at all levels of football. According to a 2019 report by the National Center for Catastrophic Sport Injury Research, there are some 4.2 million football players injured per year at all levels of the sport. From 2014 to 2019, the rate of cervical spine injuries with incomplete neurological recovery was one per one hundred thousand players. Since 1977, there have been nearly four hundred players with cervical spine injuries with incomplete neurological recovery, 80 percent occurring at the high school level and 13 percent at the collegiate level.

A little more context: 49.2 percent of players with cervical spine injuries with incomplete recovery were on the defensive side of the ball, 32.4 percent played on special teams, and only 18.4 percent were offensive players. During the same period, defensive backs (26.2 percent) and linebackers (14.3 percent) sustained the most cervical spine injuries.

Here's how these injuries break down: 54.8 percent were cervical spine fractures, 14.3 percent were cervical cord/nerve injuries, and 9.5 percent were cervical cord contusions.

As soon as I made it to Pittsburgh from Cincinnati, I learned all this medical context. I thought what had happened to me on *Monday Night Football* was another in this long series of cervical cord injuries, that my injury was no different, or maybe just different by degree, from Darryl Stingley's or Kevin Everett's or Marc Buoniconti's. But Dr. O had a bombshell to drop on me.

"No one has ever had this injury before," Dr. O said, sounding surprised himself. "Your injury has never been reported before in the history of football. In and of itself, it's a remarkable story."

Dr. O started tutoring me on what made my injury different from all those that had come before. Almost all spinal cord injuries in football center on the neck. That's why Dr. O and all team personnel practice a specific protocol every year in preparation for an on-field cervical injury. They use a special tool to remove the helmet, so as not to jar the injured area, and they immobilize the neck.

With me, there was none of that, because the impact

of my collision didn't manifest at the neck. Why? Because, Dr. O says, the force of a collision exits the body at its weakest point. And my weakest point was in my spine. Before he could even say anything further, I knew why my spine was my weak spot. I knew where Dr. O was heading—back in time, to another of those obstacles that was thrown in my way. Back to when I was a sophomore in high school and I heard for the *first* time from a doctor that I might not ever play football again.

* * *

"Ryan, I have some bad news."

Trust me, you never want to hear that from a doc. In middle school, I'd been diagnosed with scoliosis— curvature of the spine—but it was a slight case, or at least so we had been told at the time.

Now, as a high school sophomore with budding plans for a college and pro football career, I was hearing a different message. "Your scoliosis is pretty bad," the doctor said. "You're probably not going to be able to play contact sports again. You may need surgery."

It's funny when I look back on that moment now. I was staring at scoliosis ending my career before it had begun, but if you had told me then that I'd get to play this game that I dreamed about all day for the next twelve years, that I'd be a collegiate All-American and an NFL All-Pro, I'd have asked: *Where do I sign for that deal?* And if you'd added that, at twenty-seven, I'd have an injury that might keep me from ever walking again…well, you guessed it. I'd still have said, *Sign me up.*

That might sound crazy, but it's a sign of what my positive nature was like even then. If you told me I *might* never walk again, my natural inclination would be to focus on what you didn't tell me: that I *might* walk again. All I'd hear would be that I had a chance. Besides, Mom and Dad were always preaching about the power of faith. Well, I knew, deep in my bones, that God had put me on earth to play football. How could He *also* have given me a physical deformity that would keep that from happening?

Don't get me wrong, I was devastated when that doc said my scoliosis might end my career so early in high school. *You mean this game that I've loved since Dad first threw me a ball at five years old might be taken from me?* It didn't seem fair. On the way home, I sobbed. I remember looking at my mom behind the wheel, and tears were running down her cheeks. She must have felt so helpless at that moment. But not for long. Instead, she showed me what perseverance looks like. We went to, not one, but two other doctors for second and third opinions. Among the three of them there was no consensus that I'd have to give up the game—which to me would have felt like giving up my life before I'd even had the chance to really start it.

Mom made it clear that if I wasn't going to give up

the game, I had to adopt a plan for success—and I had to stick to it. This would require serious commitment. It meant sleeping every night upright and on my right, thanks to a body sculpting contraption that pulled one shoulder down, trying to right the curve in my spine. I wore the body sculptor under my clothes to school, taking it off to practice and play.

It was a bulky and annoying thing to have to wear, but if it meant I could play ball, I wasn't about to complain. By the time I got to college, the body sculptor brace was, thankfully, long gone. As far as I was concerned, I'd overcome the threat of scoliosis to my career...right?

But now here was Dr. O, showing me MRI and CT images of the curvature of my spine and walking me through just how vulnerable it made me to cervical injury. Dr. O explained that, in a patient with a spinal curvature, an anatomic weakness can develop at the apex of the curve, on the inside, or concavity, of the spine. Turns out that the bones on the inside of a spinal curve, as opposed to the outside, tend to be smaller and weaker.

That weakness was, in effect, an invitation for the force of a collision to do some serious damage. The weakest spot in most players is in their neck, which is why virtually all spinal cord injuries on the field are neck related. But the weakness left by my scoliosis made me susceptible lower down on my spine, and the impact of my collision found my most vulnerable spot. Which explained my hairline spinal fracture right at the apex of my curve.

"Before this, if someone had asked me if it was safe for a teenager with scoliosis to play football, I would have said yes," Dr. O said. "But now your case has got me rethinking that."

* * *

An hour before my surgery on Wednesday night, December 6—just forty-eight hours after my injury— my dad pulled Dr. O aside.

"Who is doing this surgery?" he wanted to know.

"Myself and Dr. Maroon," Dr. O said.

"Can you get Dr. Maroon? I need to speak to both of you," Dad said.

Once Maroon arrived, Dad huddled up close to both doctors, looking them hard in their eyes. "It don't matter to me what you believe in," he said, grabbing their hands. "I have to pray over you before you operate on my son." And right there in that hospital hallway, the three men bowed their heads while Dad blessed their hands and their hearts. When he looked up, there were tears in his eyes.

This was all happening so quickly. In a matter of days, I'd gone from being an NFL All-Pro to undergoing surgery to, hopefully, cure my paralysis. But I was raring to go. There was no angst. If the only way to get better was to have surgery, then bring it on.

Once they opened me up, Dr. O and Dr. Maroon sought to do a few things. First, they needed to stabilize my spine. So a series of screws and rods were inserted to help hold the spinal bones together and in place. Next, they excavated any spinal disc material that had ruptured into the spinal canal as a result of the injury. Finally, they drained the blood clot and drilled away some of the bone near it in order to relieve the pressure the clot had been putting on my spine.

A couple of weeks after the surgery, I'd be transferred to UPMC Mercy, an inpatient rehab center, to begin the long road back. But first, a stream of docs came to see me in my room at UPMC. One—I don't even remember her name—told me two things that might seem to be in conflict: that the surgery had been a success, and that I had maybe a 20 percent chance of ever walking again. I must not have been getting it, because I remember her saying, "We think you're done playing football, Ryan."

That doc was just doing her job, I know—giving it to me straight. But I'd already learned to bank on Dr. O, and he wasn't shutting the door on my ever playing again. "We don't really know anything," he said to me at one point. "We try as hard as we can. There are some things I can control and a giant list of things I can't. It would be the height of arrogance to presume that I know what will be possible for you in two years."

He'd also seen firsthand just how many spinal

cord injury patients end up suffering from depression and hopelessness. He'd seen how important short-, medium-, and long-term goals were to the recovery process. He knew that the odds were against my ever playing again, but he also knew that pursuing my dream would give me something to strive for and could only help me in the long run.

When they heard that doctor say I only had a 20 percent chance of walking again, Michelle and my parents turned away. I found out later just how many nights they spent sobbing, trying to wrap their heads around this terrible verdict. Me? I don't know if it was my positivity or just plain old denial, but I didn't share their despair. I thought my odds weren't that bad. Now, at least, I knew what I was up against. *Twenty percent? You mean two of every ten people in this position walk again? Okay, now I have my goal. I know what I gotta do. I gotta put together a game plan.*

Dr. O had explained to me that the spinal cord was like an electrical grid with all these circuits running through it that control strength, movement, and feeling. Well, the trauma of my injury rendered a bunch of my circuits either dead or just asleep. My job now was to do everything I could to jolt those sleeping circuits awake.

Once they put me in a wheelchair to transfer me over to UPMC Mercy, Michelle and my folks might have been scared. But I felt like I was bursting out of the locker room, ready to do battle.

CHAPTER FOUR

THE OBSTACLE IN THE PATH BECOMES THE PATH

When you watch a game of football on TV, you see a bunch of guys running around like maniacs, trying to hit one another, right? It looks uncontrolled, chaotic, and violent. Well, it *is* violent, but what appears to be haphazard is actually *planned*. The week leading up to all that on-field frenzy consists of daily meetings in which players and coaches devour all the information we can on our opponent in order to put together a game plan and control for every possible contingency.

That's why I believe football prepares you for everything in life: because it's all about planning, yes, but also about how to handle the unexpected. Every week, something happens in real time on that field— a fumble, a penalty, a blocked punt, an injury—that seemingly kicks your strategy to the curb. As a player, your job is to react to each variable in a way that still advances your game plan.

Well, postsurgery, that's where my head was at. I needed to game plan this thing out. How did I make it in college and the pros? By working, man. One day in my rookie season with the Steelers, safety Mike Mitchell said to me, "Hey, Ryan, I'll be watching film in the morning, at around eight. Stop by and I'll show you how to break down film."

That's how it started. I'd work out at 7 a.m. and then watch film with Mike in the team's scout room for an hour before our 9 a.m. team meeting. It was really impactful. He'd freeze the frame and scribble down notes on the opposing offense's tendencies. The only problem was that Mike was a defensive back, so all we were watching were pass plays. I'm a linebacker, so I have to be prepared for the running game, too. But Mike wasn't hearing any talk of expanding the playlist.

"You get here before me and you can control the remote control," he said, laughing, busting my chops. But I took it as a challenge.

My best friend and trainer, Jerome—God bless his ass—was up for getting in the gym real early. Like, *real* early. We'd work out at 4:45 a.m. so I could be at the facility by 6 a.m. to watch film by myself. Often it was just me and head coach Mike Tomlin in the building, chatting by the coffee machine and going about our business.

The only way I knew to be successful on Sunday was to feel more committed and more prepared than the eleven guys on the other side of the line of scrimmage. Now my opponent was paralysis. I knew that the only chance I had to walk and play football again was to work as hard as anyone who has ever been paralyzed.

That's why, when my docs would come in to see me, I'd assault them with questions. I was looking for data to enter into my game plan. What did I have to do? When did I have to do it by?

There's this exam they give spinal cord patients called the ASIA (American Spinal Injury Association) impairment scale. Man, I doubt they had anybody ask as many questions as often as I did about my ASIA score. See, if your exam finds you to be an A on the ASIA scale, that means you have no sensory or motor function. If you score a B, you have some sensation below the level of your injury. If you're a C, you have some muscle movement below the injury, but more than half of your muscles below the injury can't move against gravity. If you're a D, more than half of the muscles below the injury *can* move against gravity. And if you're found to be an E, you're good to go: all neurological function has been returned.

So what was I in the days after my surgery? Some movement started to come back. I was, I was told, between a C and a B. I had some minor muscle movement, but if you lifted my leg and then let go, it would just plop back down, lifeless.

I learned that most Bs don't walk again. So now I was able to see what my goal needed to be. "Aren't you a curious guy?" Dr. Maroon said one day as I threw question after question at him. Because now I had my goal: to get to a D. All those years in school, I'd never wanted a D on a test so badly.

My doctors were surprised by my intensity and my questions, but they shouldn't have been. This was me, watching film, devising a game plan.

Still, it was super easy to get distracted—by my own thoughts, for one. I couldn't quite believe all this had happened. One day, a world-class athlete, and the next, unable to walk or go to the bathroom by myself? Seriously?

But, again, football: on the field, when something ain't working, you don't have time for self-pity. "Okay," you say to yourself, "whatchu gonna do now?" That's what I had to do now, I knew. For two decades, I'd had coaches preaching the wisdom of shutting out all distractions and just focusing on the task at hand. Now, instead of that task being a tackle, it was the long, slow process of recovering from paralysis.

The other distraction was something I remain very grateful for. I still don't think I have words to adequately express the outpouring of love I felt from complete strangers. It still fills me up, man. Now, thinking back on it, I'm convinced that my initial positive attitude had a lot to do with the support I was feeling.

I'd flick on the TV and the local news would be filled with stories of fans holding prayer parties for me. Think of that: whole groups of people—strangers— were getting together to pray…for *me*. In downtown Pittsburgh, a giant "Get Well Soon, Ryan!" card was erected, and there was footage of folks lined up to sign it. And not just local Steelers fans, either. Once I saw a couple from Belgium talking about why they felt the need to sign the card. "He's so inspiring," the woman said. "I just know he's going to walk again."

And it didn't let up, either. For the next four years, I had perfect strangers coming up to me, moved. Once a young man in a wheelchair told me I was motivating him to face every new morning. Another time, an elderly white grandma saw me, burst into tears, and threw her arms around me. Clearly I had touched something in people, even if I wasn't sure what it was. Later, I'd struggle with all the attention. I *wanted* to inspire others, but I didn't want to *have* to inspire others, you know? I needed to do what I did *for* me.

At times, it became a burden, having so many people so invested in what I did. I became afraid of letting them down. Once I even called my dad and asked, "What does *'inspiration'* mean?"

He told me folks were seeing something in how I was handling what I was up against, something they could use in their own lives. "It's a blessing, son, to inspire others," he said. Thing is, I didn't know what I was doing to warrant such intense feelings from complete strangers.

Dr. O told me he'd rarely had a patient who smiled as much as me, who just did the work of recovery without complaint. Was that it? My attitude? To me, that was just second nature. It's who I was.

Even though I didn't understand it, I can't tell you how comforting it was when all those cards, flowers, texts, and social media posts first started coming my way. In the dead of night, lights off, staring at the ceiling, I'd bask in them and I wouldn't feel so alone. I'd close my eyes and just let all those prayers wash over me.

That's no figure of speech. I *felt* those prayers, like they were being applied to my skin. It might sound crazy, but I'd focus on the prayers I knew were being said for me and it would feel like my body was healing. They were making me better. When you hold hands with someone in prayer—even in a football huddle—you can feel it physically. You can feel it making you stronger. Now it felt like the greatest home field advantage in history.

"You are never more like Jesus than when you pray for others," Christian author Max Lucado wrote. I was now a part of a righteous prayerful chain that made me feel stronger than I was. I had a spiritual army behind me, made up mostly of strangers.

The Steelers have long had a unique relationship with their fans, something I'd felt even before I got hurt. In recent years, Pittsburgh may have become a tech town—Google has an office downtown, and experiments in self-driving cars take place throughout the city—but it's never really outgrown its industrial roots. It's a blue-collar city that rewards hard work and grit. When that fan base saw that I was someone who would do anything to win, when they read that I'd get to our facility to watch game film at six every morning, that I was working out every day *before* that, well, they adopted me like I'd been saying "*yinz*" my whole life.

Each day at UPMC Mercy, I was handed bags filled with cards and get-well wishes. Once there was a note from Eric LeGrand. You may remember his name. He was a defensive lineman for Rutgers University in 2010 when he suffered a spinal cord injury making a tackle on a kickoff. Lying there, he thought to himself, *I can't move. I have a full-body stinger.* Today he remains in a wheelchair, and he's a motivational speaker and author who won the Jimmy V Award for Perseverance at the ESPYs. He's also partnered with the Christopher and Dana Reeve Foundation to raise money for the fight against spinal cord injuries.

"Keep positive," Eric's note read. "Keep the faith. And work hard. Every spinal cord injury is different. None are alike. You can't listen to doctors who say you'll never walk again. They don't know."

He's right, I thought. *I'm an expert in me, and I can't let others take that away from me.* When I googled Eric, his story did something else, too: it showed me that there's life after this time of doubt and worry and fear. He's still fighting to regain feeling and hopefully walk again, but in the decade since his injury, he's built a fulfilling, rewarding life.

The same is true of Adam Taliaferro. In 2000, playing for Penn State University, he suffered a spinal cord injury and was given a 3 percent chance of walking again. When he got hurt, among the many who sent him heartfelt cards and messages was Christopher Reeve, the actor whose 1995 paralysis after an equestrian competition accident put spinal cord injuries in the public consciousness. In his 2001 book, *Miracle in the Making*, Taliaferro quotes from the note sent to him by Reeve, who died in 2004:

I heard about your injury and just wanted to drop you a note to let you know that you will get through this....I was once where you are now. It seems surreal. It seems like your life has been turned upside down. I remember being so angry that this happened to me. I remember the frustration, and especially, I remember the fear. You are done with surgery and about to begin rehabilitation. You'll learn new ways to do the same old things. Most importantly, you'll discover who you are....You should know that the Christopher Reeve Paralysis Foundation funds research for a cure. It is no longer a question of "if" but "when." So on those days when you're really down, know that hope is on the way....In the meantime, push yourself in your rehabilitation as hard as you pushed yourself for football. Let people help you. Remember that your life holds so much more than you can imagine. Keep going.

Reeves's note to Taliaferro reminded me of the best motivational speeches I've heard coaches give through the years. It was hopeful, inspiring, and challenging. When you hear someone you don't know tell you they believe in you, that they have faith in you, you stand a little taller—even if you can't stand at all. Adam must have been fired up.

A year after his injury, his football career was over, but Adam Taliaferro walked back onto the field he'd been carried off of. When he led his team out of the Penn State tunnel, the Nittany Lion faithful erupted into sustained and thunderous applause. Adam went on to found the Adam Taliaferro Foundation—a source of financial and logistical support for families dealing with spinal cord injuries—and to earn a law degree. He's now a New Jersey state assemblyman. How's that for a stirring life story?

Of course, it wasn't just strangers sending me love and showing me that this, too, shall pass. My teammates and the whole Steeler family were unbelievable. Within days of my injury, wide receiver Antonio Brown had a buddy of his design custom yellow cleats with my face on them for the guys to wear during the warm-up to our upcoming game against Baltimore.

Before my injury, those of us who played linebacker—about eight guys—started having weekly linebacker dinners together. In fact, the previous Friday night we'd gathered at Hyde Park, a popular steakhouse, for some laughs and bonding over red meat and wine. I have a photo of all of us in my phone that I'd look at from my hospital bed, a sad reminder of all that I'd suddenly lost.

But shame on me for thinking they were symbols of what I'd lost. These were my teammates, and in the NFL, as in war, that means you have a lifetime bond. My guys just moved the venue of our weekly dinners to a hospital conference room, and they brought along other guys from the defense as well. They called it our weekly team meeting, but the vibe wasn't quite that businesslike. We'd eat together, watch a game, and play video games, and they'd brief me on the game plan for Sunday. I'd know the plays the team was going to run and those of our opponent. That way, I could watch the game like a player—a teammate— and not just a fan.

Those get-togethers were really a lifeline. Often in the NFL, guys who get seriously injured kind of disappear from their team. It's hard for the player to be around his teammates when he's no longer contributing on the field, and it's hard for the players to keep seeing this reminder of the risk they run every day.

I'll treasure those hospital conference room hang-outs as long as I live. On the field, when you blow an assignment or get beat on a play, your teammates will pat you on the shoulder pad and say, "I got you." What they mean is, *I'll do something to make it up for you, because you'd do the same for me.* It's called being a team.

And that's what those hospital team meetings were all about: a weekly "I got you" from my teammates. But I wasn't surprised, because, for some reason, in the Steel City, there's something almost spiritual about the connection between you and your team-mates, and between you, your teammates, and the fans. Back in 1979—well before I was even born—baseball's Pittsburgh Pirates won a World Series and their championship theme song was *"We Are Family"* by Sister Sledge. The same could be said of every Steelers team. If you were part of Steeler Nation, you were part of a sacred bond.

The team was loyal to its players at a time when pro sports had become big, impersonal business. It wasn't lost on African American players that the Steelers have long been at the forefront of civil rights advocacy. The Steelers have been owned by the Rooney family for generations, and have long stood for equality of opportunity for both people of color and women. The Steelers were the first to hire an African American coach in modern NFL history (Lowell Perry), the first to start an African American quarterback on opening day, (Joe Gilliam Jr.), the first to have an African American Super Bowl MVP (Franco Harris), the first to hire an African American defensive coordinator (Tony Dungy), the first to hire a female trainer (Ariko Iso). The Rooney family was so committed to social justice that, when the NFL mandated that every team must interview an African American candidate when searching for a head coach, it became known as the Rooney Rule after Dan Rooney, who was the head of the league's diversity committee at the time.

That's why it wasn't surprising that my teammates remained my teammates when I was in the hospital. Some teams in the NFL are a collection of individual players. In Pittsburgh, we're all *Steelers*.

* * *

Mom, Dad, and Michelle never seemed to leave my hospital room. Dad and Mom stayed at our house. Michelle slept on a cot by my bedside, and Dad would have to convince her to take a break every once in a while and go home for a quick nap.

Even with all that support—my family staying close, my teammates showing up, the fans sending prayers and good vibes—I couldn't help but fall at times into a deep funk. In a matter of days, I'd gone from a healthy, independent man to a patient who had to rely on others for the basics in life that so many of us take for granted every day. I had to be shown how to stretch my legs. How to roll over. How to get in and out of a chair. How to put on socks. A nurse had to wash me. An orderly had to lift me from the bed to hover above a bedpan in order to move my bowels. And I urinated through a catheter that had been put in place during my surgery.

It wasn't long before I developed a urinary tract infection from the catheter. This was common, I was told, but that didn't stop me from suddenly falling into despair.

My fever spiked. Antibiotics meant to fight the infection made me sick to my stomach. That's when I threw up right in front of my cousin, Nehari Crawford, and some of the vomit bounced off the rail on the side of the bed and hit me.

I'd always been like a proud big brother to Nehari, who had recently finished his college career as Duquesne University's all-time leader in receiving yards and receptions. I hated for him to see me so sick and weak. Later I'd see the wisdom in the Eckhart Tolle quote, "All stress is about wanting the what is to be what it is not." I was suffering because I was fixated on this old image of myself—a strong warrior laying down an example for my cousin. I was obsessing over the "what is not."

But I didn't get that at the time. Instead, my positive attitude melted away and my faith was suddenly gone. Now a victim soundtrack started playing in my own head: *Why me, God? What did I do to deserve this? What did my dad—your humble servant—do to deserve this?*

Outwardly, I still kept trying to crack jokes, to keep things light for Mom, Dad, and Michelle. But behind my brave facade I was crumbling. I was depressed one moment, pissed the next.

You're sick, Ryan. That's when those images of that day in 2016 came to me, the day Michelle and Jerome and Vernon II and I were riffing on the power of *shalieving. Ya gotta Shalieve!*

I knew I needed to find my way back to problem-solving. But how? Luckily, Dad was watching me closely and sensed something was wrong. He had an idea.

* * *

"Son, you just need to string a few first downs together."

That's what my dad said, sensing how down I was. Now, I'm a defensive player—I'm built to *deny* first downs. But the more I thought about it, the more I realized Dad was pointing the way for me.

When you're down by three touchdowns late in the game, why can't you come back? Because the task seems insurmountable. That's four possessions! You can't imagine it. You start to press, as if you can make up the deficit on one big play. That's actually panic, and it invariably results in turnovers instead of a comeback.

But what if you trained yourself to take it one first down at a time? You might need four plays to get that first down, but when you do, you've achieved a reachable goal. We've all seen it: string a few of those first downs together and that momentum can feed on itself, right?

That's what Dad was talking about. He'd always taught me to be goal oriented. My ultimate goal might be to play football again, but if that were my *only* goal, my days were going to be filled with frustration and panic and depression. I needed some *reachable* goals.

Once I got past my UTI, I started my rehab. At first, I couldn't even sit up in bed. After many frustrating tries, and with help from a team of kind physical therapists, wouldn't you know it—there I was, sitting up in bed.

One physical therapist kept throwing a teddy bear at me to test my reaction time. And every time I caught that bear, there was Dad, marking the occasion in no uncertain terms.

"That's it," Dad would cry out. "That's a first down, son! Lord, thank you for this first down!"

One day I was able to shakily stand up, with some steadying help. You would have thought I'd just gone through two-a-days. I stood there, teetering.

"That's a first down, son," Dad said, welling up. "You're getting better. This is you getting better."

Now, that alone would exhaust me for a day. Merely standing up drained me. At times, that got to me. I'd always prided myself on my strength and stamina. Needing help to just stand up? And feeling wiped out by that? You kidding me?

But there was Dad, coaching me to focus on the short-term goal in front of me. In little ways, my faith walk started coming back—even if I still couldn't physically walk. Instead of being pissed that there I was, an All-Pro linebacker, and an occupational therapist was showing me how to use a clawlike device to put my damned socks on, I psyched myself up to meet the challenge of getting a first down. And when, finally, those socks made it onto my feet, it was high-five time.

"Thank you, Lord, for this first down," Dad said.

There would be so many moments like that in the months to come. The first time I was able to stand up without any help. The first time I could use the bathroom. The first time I could take a wobbly step on my own. Always, there was Dad, marking the moment: "This is you getting better," he'd say.

Once, there were other people in the room, and I motioned for Dad to come in close for a secret. He leaned over me. "I think I shit myself," I whispered. Dad didn't miss a beat.

"That means you can *feel* something, son," he said, before calling the nurse to get me cleaned up. "Your body is waking up. Thank you, Lord, for this first down!"

Yeah, he actually thanked the Lord because I crapped the bed.

One turning point that still stands out was December 16, just ten days after my surgery. It was also my brother Vernon's twenty-first birthday. Tomorrow would be my first day out in public. We'd be going to the Steelers game against the Patriots.

That afternoon, Dr. Maroon came by my room. "Let's check how you're progressing," he said. Mom, Dad, Michelle, Vernon II, and Jerome were all there.

Up until now, if someone raised either of my legs off the bed and let go, they'd plop right back down, lifeless. "Try to straighten this leg, hold it up," Dr. Maroon said, lifting my left leg up. All eyes—mine and everybody else's—were on my leg. All of us were expecting what we'd seen for the last two weeks: a log-like leg. Instead, there it was, hovering an inch off the bed, as if it were struggling for life itself. I don't know how long I kept that leg airborne—twenty seconds?—but in those seconds, a room full of adults was filled with hope and a sense of God's grace.

Now Michelle and Mom and Dad let me see them cry, because these were tears of belief and joy. "Good Lord," Dad said, "that's not a first down. That's your first touchdown!"

The next day, there I was at Heinz Field. During warm-ups before the game, I was taken out onto the field, where my teammates mobbed me. On our way back inside the stadium, fans swarmed my wheelchair. We watched the game from the luxury box of my friend Thomas Tull, part owner of the Steelers. Thomas is a billionaire businessman and movie producer who executive-produced movies like *The Hangover*, *The Dark Knight*, and *Straight Outta Compton*. For all his success, Thomas is one of the most down-to-earth guys I know.

During a time-out, they flashed a shot of Michelle and me on the stadium's video screen, and I raised my Terrible Towel and, with an ear-to-ear grin, waved it like what I was: a rabid member of Steeler Nation. The place went wild. It wasn't about the game or the score. I felt what it was about: pure love. It washed over me.

I don't know if my appearance at the game fired up the guys, but we came out ballin'. Antonio Brown got hurt and had to leave the game, but we led until the final minutes of the fourth quarter. Brady gave the Pats a 27–24 lead with fifty-six seconds remaining, but Big Ben put some big plays together and hit Jesse James with what appeared to be the game-winning touchdown with thirty-four seconds left. But, even though no defensive player so much as touched him, the referee ruled the pass incomplete, saying James's control of the ball did not survive his contact with the ground. It was a mind-boggling call that flew in the face of what we'd all seen: a catch.

Coach Tomlin was diplomatic after the 27–24 loss. I was pissed at the call and bummed that we'd lost. But I also thought a lot about the warm embrace I'd felt from the crowd that day. I committed those cheers to memory, and back at rehab, I liked to imagine they were for my first downs, like when feeling came back in my legs. Ah, sensation. Who would have thought that touching your leg and feeling it would be cause for celebration? You really never know what you've got till it's gone.

Every time I got a first down, I'd hear those fans. Steeler Nation was with me all the way.

*　*　*

Most visitors to my room had been bringing flowers or boxes of chocolates or spreads of food. Not my man Thomas Tull. He pulled up a chair next to my bed and handed me a book, *The Obstacle Is the Way* by Ryan Holiday.

"I think this can really help you," he said. I leafed through the pages, and it appeared to be about some ancient philosophy called...Stoicism? Uh, count me as skeptical that this would be a page-turner. But then Thomas explained that this book, which had sold some seven hundred thousand copies and had been translated into nearly twenty languages, was the secret behind the success of coaches like Bill Belichick, Nick Saban, and Lane Kiffin. If they swore by it, who was I not to crack it open?

I found myself reading about this dude Marcus Aurelius, a second-century Roman emperor whose philosophy, Stoicism, holds that you can shape your own destiny by controlling what you can and letting go of what you can't. The key to happiness, the Stoics say, is not what happens to us; it's how we *respond* to what happens to us.

How could this way of thinking not speak to me? "The obstacle in the path becomes the path," wrote Holiday, quoting an ancient Zen monk. "Never forget, within every obstacle is an opportunity to improve our condition." Thomas was right: I needed to hear not just that there was a way to overcome my present circumstances but that my misfortune was actually an opportunity, if only I was open to it.

Among my underlined passages: "It does not matter what you bear, but how you bear it." That was from the ancient Roman philosopher Seneca, who used to say he pitied people who had it too easy.

And: "You have passed through life without an opponent," Seneca said. "No one can ever know what you are capable of, not even you."

Whoa. I couldn't put the book down, highlighting passages that made me want to get out of bed and pile first down upon first down in order to show the kind of man I am. When I read that the great Stoic Epictetus said, "It is impossible for a man to learn what he thinks he already knows," I realized I *am* a Stoic. I just never knew it before.

Holiday, the author, had had his own Stoic awakening. He'd been the marketing director of the controversial American Apparel brand, which became mired in sexual harassment scandals and damaged by the frat boy demeanor of its corporate bosses. Holiday heeded Aurelius's advice, however—"Waste no more time arguing what a good man should do. Be one."—and remade himself into a best-selling author who applied ancient philosophies to modern-day life.

When he walked the reader through Alabama coach Nick Saban's Stoic approach, I could have sworn he was speaking directly to me.

> In the chaos of sport, as in life, process provides us a way. It says: Okay, you've got to do something very difficult. Don't focus on that. Instead break it down into pieces. Simply do what you need to do right now. . . . Excellence is a matter of steps. Excelling at this one, then that one, and then the one after that. Saban's process is exclusively this—existing in the present, taking it one step at a time, not getting distracted by anything else. Not the other team, not the scoreboard or the crowd. . . . Whether it's pursuing the pinnacle of success in your field or simply surviving some awful or trying ordeal, the same approach works. Don't think about the end—think about surviving. Making it from meal to meal, break to break, checkpoint to checkpoint, paycheck to paycheck, one day at a time.

Yes! It ain't about *what* happens to you—it's about how you *think about* what happens to you.

*The phrase "This happened and it is bad" is actually two
impressions. The first—"This happened"—is objective.
The second—"it is bad"—is subjective. The sixteenth-
century Samurai swordsman Miyamoto Musashi won
countless fights against feared opponents, even multiple
opponents, in which he was swordless. In* The Book of
Five Rings, *he notes the difference between observing
and perceiving. The perceiving eye is weak, he wrote;
the observing eye is strong. Musashi understood that the
observing eye sees simply what is there. The perceiving
eye sees more than what is there.*

The idea that in every obstacle lies opportunity was
just what I needed to hear. If I spent too much time
feeling sorry for myself or worrying about whether
I'd walk or play football again, I'd be wasting energy
on things beyond my control. What I could control
was what I did every single minute of every day.

That meant practicing what the Stoics called the
art of acquiescence: "When a doctor gives you orders
or a diagnosis—even if it's the opposite of what
you wanted—what do you do?" Holiday wrote. "You
accept it. You don't have to like or enjoy the treatment
but you know that denying it only delays the cure."

Now, mind you, this doesn't mean giving up. It
means facing what is, so you can fight *smart*. I had to
embrace that I was no longer that All-Pro linebacker,
bouncing on my toes, ready to pounce.

Thanks to the fans, my teammates, my mom, my

dad, Michelle, Vernon, Jerome, and the Stoics, that was becoming easier to do. Any tendency toward bitterness or self-pity was fading away. No wonder coaches like Belichick loved Holiday's book: football offers a similar lesson. The only way to get better is to focus with intensity on the task at hand.

I was so moved by Holiday's book that I tracked him down for a couple of heart-to-hearts over the phone. He was smart and full of compassion. His writings, and my conversations with him, inspired me to get more and more first downs in rehab. And, just as Aurelius advised centuries ago, they also made me want to be a better man.

CHAPTER FIVE
"I'M NOT GOING ANYWHERE"

Something had been weighing on me, something I'd been putting off. Every night, Mom and Dad would leave the hospital, and Michelle would curl up on that uncomfortable cot. And every night, I'd feel pangs of guilt for what I was putting her through.

We weren't married yet, after all. I was already a dad—my son, Ryan Jr. (R.J.), who was three when I got injured, lived with his mom in Columbus, Ohio, and spent his summers with me. But Michelle, who was great with R.J. and who loved kids, wasn't yet a mom. And I knew that was a dream of hers.

I'd read enough about the after-effects of paralysis to know the burdens shouldered by the caregivers. I felt like I couldn't be selfish about this. I loved Michelle with all my heart. That might mean having to let her go.

One night, after Mom and Dad had gone, Michelle came out of the bathroom and got ready for bed.

"Can we talk?" I said.

* * *

Flash back to October of 2015. I was missing R.J. It was midseason, so I was in Pittsburgh. I hadn't seen my little buddy in a few months. I was looking through photos of him and posted one of his baby pictures on my Instagram page.

Little did I know that in San Antonio, Texas, a young woman who loved baby pics would come across R.J.'s photo. I noticed that someone named Michelle Rodriguez liked what I'd posted. On her Instagram Explore page, there were many baby photos, including the one I'd posted of R.J. Now, I'm not gonna lie: she looked *hot* in the photo on her page. I thought she was beautiful, and I couldn't stop thinking of her smiling face.

"I was looking through your page and couldn't help but notice your beautiful smile," I wrote to her.

"Thank you," she replied.

"My name's Ryan," I wrote. "It's nice to meet you."

It took her a minute to put together that I was the dad of one of the babies whose picture she'd included on her feed. And then we just started connecting. From the get-go, I felt like I could be myself with Michelle. I didn't have to front.

It started with us sharing our favorite Bible verses.

Mine, I told her, was Psalm 23, which I read before practice every day:

The Lord is my shepherd; I shall not want.
He maketh me to lie down in green pastures: he leadeth
me beside the still waters.
He restoreth my soul: he leadeth me in the paths of
righteousness for his name's sake.
Yea, though I walk through the valley of the shadow of
death, I will fear no evil: for thou art with me; thy
rod and thy staff they comfort me.

Why that verse? It went back to what Dad had always preached when I was growing up. You're never alone, not really. God is with you, if only you believe. I was a young, single star athlete—that's a lot of pressure to face on your own. I'd read Psalm 23 every day and not feel so alone.

I'd never been so open and vulnerable with someone, especially someone I hadn't even met yet. But there was something about Michelle—she *invited* openness. Soon, messages over social media led to phone calls, which led to long FaceTime conversations. And by "long," I mean sometimes all night.

On January 9, 2016, my Steelers took on the Cincinnati Bengals in the AFC wild card playoff game. In the third quarter, Bengals running back Giovani Bernard caught a screen pass and turned to run upfield. But he ran into a buzz saw named Shazier. I hit him at full

70

force, leading with my helmet—this was before the NFL outlawed head-to-head tackling. It was a clean hit; no flag was thrown because Bernard had turned and was no longer a defenseless player. He was trying to advance the football.

But I hit him square—tackling *through* the runner, as Dad had preached—and knocked him out cold, forcing a fumble. For a while, Giovani lay motionless on the ground. He left the game and entered the league's concussion protocol. Cincinnati fans and players were livid; they thought a penalty should have been called on the play. Fans started pelting the field with trash and beer cups. A chippy game grew even chippier. Afterward, I tweeted out a message to Bernard, who also comes from the Sunshine State: "Never been out to hurt ppl. Praying @G_Bernard25 recovers well. Respect you as a player and love playing against you. #Respect #Lauderdale."

What I didn't mention in that tweet or any of the postgame interviews (we ended up winning a crazy game with a last-second field goal) was that I'd been up practically the whole night before the game, talking to Michelle.

Sometimes we'd fall asleep together while on the phone. My teammates were giving me all sorts of business about this new relationship. Remember, I still hadn't met Michelle in person—and we'd been talking for, like, three months, often multiple times a day. Some of my teammates teased me that she wasn't even real—that I was being catfished. ("That's why FaceTime is great!" I'd reply.) Others warned me that things were getting real serious, real quick.

"You better watch out, Ryan," the guys said. "Or you gonna marry this girl."

I couldn't help it; I just loved learning everything about her. Michelle was twenty-four and had been raised in San Antonio by her parents, Felix and Zoraida, transplants from Puerto Rico with whom she still lived.

When we first started talking, Michelle didn't even know I was a pro athlete, but I soon got the sense that she understood what it takes to excel in sports. She'd played high school basketball, where she was a baller, playing in the Senior Alamo All-Star game. She played one season at the University of Texas at Arlington before transferring to Texas State University and focusing on her studies, but she remained a hoop head. After we met in person, I'd fly out to San Antonio once a month and we'd invariably go to a Spurs game, where she clued me in on the supreme skill of Kawhi Leonard, long before he became an NBA superstar.

Given how much Michelle loved kids, I wasn't surprised to learn she was a special education teacher. I remember talking to her for hours about R.J. and her saying how excited she'd be to meet him one day.

Our 2016 season ended in a heartbreaker against Denver in the AFC Championship Game. Peyton

Manning performed his old late-game magic, leading the Broncos on a game-winning drive. I had seven tackles—six solo—but we lost, 23–16, to the eventual Super Bowl champions. But the close of my season had a silver lining: I invited Michelle to Pittsburgh so we could finally meet in person.

She was a good, God-fearing girl who was very close with her parents, and they didn't know about me. So she told them she was going to Dallas when she was actually headed to Pittsburgh to spend the weekend with a pro athlete. Once she got to the Burgh, she experienced snow for the first time in her life. We joined my brother and his girlfriend on a ski trip, ate some great meals, and got to know each other even better. After that, she came clean to her parents about me, and soon I was visiting San Antonio and staying with them, often for a week at a time during my off-season.

* * *

But my off-season that year wasn't *all* about Michelle. Right after that playoff loss to Peyton Manning and the Broncos, Coach Tomlin cried in the locker room. Seeing how much our leader cared—man, that fired me up. I had to ask myself: *What else can I do to get better?*

Given that I'd missed games because of a concussion and a shoulder injury, and that I'd soon be undergoing arthroscopic knee surgery, I knew the answer. I had to figure out how to stay healthy during the grind of an NFL season.

My teammate James Harrison was an imposing physical specimen. The dude was in his late thirties and still dominated the line of scrimmage. He was a five-time Pro Bowler and the Steelers' all-time sacks leader, with eighty. He introduced me to his personal trainer, Ian Danney, whose company—PEP, for Performance Enhancement Professionals—took elite athletes through a comprehensive program that included training, nutrition, and performance therapy. Ian didn't mess around, and I went out to his facility in Scottsdale, Arizona, to learn from him.

But I didn't go alone. I couldn't spend the whole off-season in Arizona because I wanted to be with R.J. So my man Jerome Howard came out with me. Ian agreed not just to train me but also to take Jerome under his wing and teach him how to implement the PEP system as a trainer.

Jerome and I had been best friends since eighth grade and were teammates at Plantation High, where he played linebacker. We went our separate ways after high school, me to Ohio State, him to Prairie View A&M University. There, he dominated as a four-year starter; he was a two-time All-American and the 2015 SWAC Defensive Player of the Year, and he still holds the Prairie View record for career tackles.

Injuries kept Jerome from making it at the pro level,

but he put his athletic background and bachelor's degree in human performance to good use. He was training athletes back in Florida when I called to see if he'd be into making the trip to Scottsdale to study under Ian and then come back with me to Pittsburgh and be my trainer. It was a heavy ask—*Will you uproot your whole life and come work with me?*—but Jerome was all over it. "Bro, whatever you need," he said. "I'm down."

Ian was blown away by Jerome's intensity. Later, back in Pittsburgh, Jerome and I became Team Shazier, hitting the gym every morning at 4:45 a.m. before I'd watch film at the team's facility. Jerome was not just a trainer; he was a coach and motivator, too, as when we came up with that slogan: *Ya Gotta Shalieve!*

The thing about all that work was that it didn't feel like work. When it's just you and your bro and you're challenging each other every day to do one more rep, when you're good-naturedly talking smack, it's not a job—it's a passion.

And speaking of passion: in April 2016, I flew Michelle out to Scottsdale for a few weeks during my training. We stayed at the luxurious Sanctuary Camelback Mountain Resort and Spa. We'd lounge by the infinity pool, dine on the American cuisine of chef and *Food Network* star Beau MacMillan while looking out on a breathtaking desert vista, and go for walks in the property's Zen meditation garden and by the soothing reflection pond. She didn't know it, but I'd already talked to Michelle's parents and mine: I was planning on proposing.

I took her to a nice restaurant—she hates getting all dressed up, so it took some persuading. Once there, we saw a photographer taking pictures of a model under a tree. Little did Michelle know this was all a setup. He told us he was new to the photography game and was practicing his craft.

"Well, if it helps you out, you can take some photos of us," I said.

The sun was setting as he started clicking away. That's when I dropped to one knee. We have photos of Michelle's hands covering her mouth in surprise as she realized just what was about to go down.

We still hadn't known each other long, so, as we celebrated that night, I made it clear that I recognized this was all happening fast and that we could do this on her timetable. "I know you're from a close-knit family," I told her, "and I want to make sure they know how serious I am about you, and us."

Within a few months, we were rolling. Michelle hired a wedding planner and picked out a dress and caterer. We settled on a date and location: July 7, 2018, in Miami, which would be convenient for my family and so many of her relatives who'd be coming from Puerto Rico.

But then *Monday Night Football* in Cincinnati happened. What's that old saying? *Man plans, and God laughs.*

* * *

Now here we were, in my room at UPMC Mercy, and it was time to acknowledge a couple of elephants in the room. First, I had to broach the subject of postponing the wedding. I couldn't imagine being in the right frame of mind for such a joyous occasion in just six months. "I don't want to look back at pictures of my wedding years from now and see myself in a wheelchair, looking unhappy," I said. "This is supposed to be one of the happiest days of our lives, getting married, and I don't want to look back and think, if we had waited a little bit more, I would have been a lot better and I would have been on my feet, walking, dancing, jumping."

We held hands. She got it. "We're going to dance at *our* wedding," she said.

Now came the hard part. I'd been coaching myself for this moment. *If you truly love her, you want what's best for her,* I kept telling myself.

I told her how much I loved her, but that I'd been reading about the demands that are placed on the caregiver of a paralysis patient. The caregiver often feels isolated, robbed of personal time, exhausted, and overwhelmed. Caregivers have to deal with medical concerns, matters of hygiene, transportation, advocacy, and, potentially, end-of-life issues.

Michelle hadn't signed up for any of this. For life with someone who might never walk again. For a marriage that, for all we knew, could be sexless and childless. My heart was breaking.

"You're a beautiful twenty-six-year-old woman," I said, holding her hand. "You don't deserve any of this. I may be paralyzed, I may be totally dependent on you. I understand if you don't want to deal with this."

My girl didn't miss a beat.

"I told you I was going to marry you no matter what," Michelle said, squeezing my hand. "I'm not going anywhere. I don't care if I have to wheel you down the aisle or push you around for the rest of your life. I've got your back."

I've got your back. I can still hear those words, and they still move me. That girl's got more heart than sense. I was at my most vulnerable, and despite my positive outlook, a part of me was terrified about the road ahead. To hear the woman you love affirm that she's going to be on that road with you? Man, how lucky could one guy be?

CHAPTER SIX

RECOVERY ROAD

A few days before our divisional playoff game against the Jacksonville Jaguars, I went to practice. I sat in my wheelchair on the sideline—but the way my teammates and coaches treated me, it was like I'd be suiting up come Sunday. They swarmed me with hugs and high fives, sure, but the thing that really touched me was that I was *included* in the substance of the practice. Any talk of game planning, and I was part of that conversation.

When I got home, I posted this on Instagram:

I want to thank the Lord for the first downs that he has been allowing me to achieve. The touchdown is going to come in His timing, but today was a first down. I was finally able to make it to practice with my teammates. It's great to be back for practices and meetings. Just to be able to feel a part of it means the world. So I'm working harder than I ever have to get back. I've been making strides over the past month and continue to make progress. Taking it day-by-day, but I'm far from done. The Lord has not finished his work yet. I want to say thank you to the fans and Steelers Nation for the prayers. If it wasn't for my family, friends and your prayers I wouldn't be where I am now. They have lifted me and my family through this journey and I ask for you to continue praying for me, as I continue to work daily on improving my health. #Shalieve #Steelers #prayfor50

Among the many messages posted in response was this:

The heart of a fucking lion. Watching you learn how to walk all over again after ur injury inspired me to do the same as I was paralyzed may 1, 2019 from injury where the er dr didn't help me in time so lost mobility in my lower half for 3 weeks…I have been rehabbing and battling…Keep inspiring thank you @shazier

I was fired up. Come Sunday, there I was, leading the cheering from the stands during our home play-off game, wearing a "#50 Shalieve" sweatshirt we'd had designed. "I've fought my hardest to be a leader and a force on the field for Pittsburgh, bleeding black and gold on the front lines," I wrote on Instagram on game day.

Pittsburgh has embraced me—and I have embraced it back. It truly is a place like no other. Over the last few weeks, my family and I have tasked [Pittsburgh Proud Athletic Clothes and Accessories] Shop 412 with a very important job—to create a design with me that would show our city how much drive and passion I have for it. I wanted to make something that could serve as a representation of my spirit, of my inner fight, and also be a creative way to bring some fire to my squad and to our fans as we head proudly into these playoffs.

A lot of my teammates wore the shirt during warm-ups, but it didn't deliver what I'd hoped: though we were favored to win, we lost in a shoot-out, 45–42. Ben did what he could, throwing for five touchdowns and passing for nearly five hundred yards. But in the fourth quarter, Jacksonville quarterback Blake Bortles did a Tom Brady impression. The Steelers led the NFL with fifty-five sacks, but we couldn't get to Bortles once.

Afterward, I couldn't help feeling like I let my teammates down by not being lined up alongside them that day. I read in the newspaper that we'd only allowed two one-hundred-yard runners in the twelve games I'd been in the lineup, but three in the five games since. And we'd given up 28 points per game since I'd been out, up from 17.5—a stunning 60 percent jump.

For a moment after that loss, my mind was hijacked by those "what if" thoughts. *What if I hadn't gotten hurt? What if it had just been a stinger? What if I hadn't played in that Monday night game, as Michelle had suggested? I could have been on the field in a playoff game, helping my teammates.*

But by now I was learning to refocus. As an athlete, I had always used self-talk. *He can't stick you*, I'd tell myself about the running back who was charged with blocking me. But now I was learning how to use *distanced* self-talk to quiet my racing thoughts. In his book *Chatter: The Voice in Our Head, Why It Matters, and How to Harness It*, Ethan Kross, a University of Michigan professor and director of the Emotion and Self-Control Laboratory, explains that using distanced language—speaking to yourself as if you're somebody else—can help you turn a perceived threat into a challenge, a negative into a positive. In other words, you can be your own coach. "Distanced self-talk can be the pivotal shove that sends you down the path of the challenge mindset," he writes.

Here's where I'd call upon my old friends, the Stoics, quoting Epictetus to myself as if I weren't this guy who was suddenly down in the dumps because he wasn't on the football field: *Ryan, remember, the more we value things outside our control, the less control we have.*

Repeat that, mantra-like, for a few minutes and the next step is inevitable: you train yourself to focus on what you *can* control. And, I kept telling myself, I could control coming back to walk *and* play again.

* * *

A little more than a month after my injury, I was still blown away by how the Steelers had reacted. Coach Mike Tomlin—whom I had come to see as a type of father figure—checked in with me almost every day. And when they put me on the injured reserve list, I didn't hear about it on talk radio. Instead, general manager Kevin Colbert visited me personally for a very cool conversation.

Kevin had been the GM in Pittsburgh since 2000, so, along with owner Dan Rooney and his son Art Rooney II, the Steelers' president, Kevin was an integral part of the brain trust behind the city's two most recent Super Bowl wins. That's two of the franchise's *six* rings, tied with New England for the most ever.

In case you've forgotten: in Super Bowl XL, Bill Cowher coached the Steelers to a 21–10 win over Seattle, behind my man "Big Ben" Roethlisberger and MVP wide receiver Hines Ward. And in Super Bowl XLIII, it was Tomlin leading the team to victory over the Arizona Cardinals, 23–16, behind Ben and another wide receiver MVP, Santonio Holmes.

Since I was drafted in 2014, Kevin and I had built up a great relationship. I'd always trained to be a warrior before my injury, so I might never have heard the term "emotional intelligence" until I was in the hospital and Googling what it takes to recover from trauma. It's defined as "the capacity to be aware of, control, and express one's emotions, and to handle interpersonal relationships judiciously and empathetically." *Holy crap*, I thought. *That describes Kevin.*

He knows athletes, knows what makes us tick. And he knows the Burgh, having grown up not far from Three Rivers Stadium in the city's North Side. He attended North Catholic High School and then stayed local at Robert Morris University.

At a time when the trend in sports was to hire Ivy League nerds who swear by analytics for the front office, Colbert was a Pittsburgh guy *and* a football guy. He'd been a collegiate assistant basketball coach and head baseball coach, too, so he knew the psyche of the athlete.

"I want you to understand that I know it's going to be a long journey back," Kevin said when he came to see me. "No matter what, we've got your back until you say you're done."

Man, there was that phrase again: *got your back.* "That really means a lot, man," I said.

"We want you back," Kevin said. "And we'll do

everything in our power to let whatever happens be *your* choice."

After my first Pro Bowl selection in 2016, the Steelers had picked up my $8.7 million fifth-year option heading into the 2017 season. Now, they would put me on the reserve/physically unable to perform list and convert about $8.2 million of that money into a signing bonus for salary cap purposes and then toll my contract in 2018—meaning the contract would be put on hold and transferred to the next year's books. They'd continue providing my medical insurance and, if need be, Kevin said, they'd toll my contract again the following year—he just wanted to be sure to give me enough space to fully explore coming back.

Do you know how rare it is to hear something like that from your GM in the NFL? Players like to call the NFL the "Not For Long" league because, when a guy gets injured, his team quickly moves on to the next dude. You hear coaches and players reference that "next man up" mentality all the time. I get it, and I've always gotten it. An NFL franchise is a high-stakes operation. There are business pressures behind every decision. I used to laugh when guys in the locker room would bitch and complain about how the team didn't do right by them come contract time—they'd talk about it in the most personal terms. "Man, I thought me and Kevin were cool," they might say.

I've seen teams make bad personnel decisions, but I've never thought they were made based on emotion.

Teams have to make tough calls about what is best for the organization as a whole. As a leader of the team, I had to tell a teammate more than once, "Bro, it just might not make sense for them to keep you."

So I get that the game is a business. But I think one of the reasons the Steelers have been so successful through the years is that it's not *just* a business to folks like Kevin. A little emotional intelligence goes a long way. I'm convinced that one of the reasons the Steelers have been so good for so long is that they treat people like people.

If you work for the Rooneys, you're not just a number. And that's known throughout the league. I've talked to many opposing players who want to play in the Burgh because they're dying to be appreciated by the guys who sign their paycheck.

Here's a perfect example from a couple of months after that initial conversation with Kevin. Leading up to the NFL Draft, Kevin stopped by to see me while Jerome and I were working out. "I wanted to run something by you," he said. "There's a possibility we may draft a linebacker. How would that make you feel?"

Seriously? Are you asking about my feelings right now? "I knew that would be a possibility," I said. "But I gotta say, I really respect you for talking to me about it."

Like a Stoic, I told Kevin I could only control what I could control, and that was how much blood, sweat, and tears I was dripping on the gym floor every morning. The team ended up *not* drafting a line-backer, which made me feel great. That meant they were cool with waiting a year to see how my recovery went. And it meant that I'd work even harder to get back. Because if Kevin Colbert had my back, then I'd have his. And I'd have run through brick walls for that dude.

Kevin's faith in me fired me up so much that I made my first public comments since the injury, on my teammate Roosevelt Nix's podcast.

Up till then, only my friends and family knew I was determined to play again. I didn't expect some comments on a podcast to blow up, but they did.

"I've got to get back," I said, before referencing the Stoics. "Right now I'm reading a book, and it's basically saying trust the process. I'm really trusting the process. I know the end goal. So I'm taking every step of the way; I'm giving everything I got. The therapists are like, 'Man, this is crazy; I've never seen anyone work this hard.' They see progression almost every day."

Remember how, when I was growing up, Dad used to have me identify my goals *and* the steps I was willing to take to attain them? Well, I was still doing it. And last season, before getting injured, I'd written down a pair of pretty audacious goals: to play for seventeen years—just like legendary linebacker Ray Lewis—and be a first-ballot Hall of Famer. Well, I was so comfortable talking to my man Nix, who had been a linebacker before making the transition to fullback, that I didn't think twice about sharing them.

"I'm still reaching for that Hall of Fame because I really feel I'm the best linebacker ever," I said.

I didn't expect comments made on Roosevelt Nix's podcast to become a big story, but Twitter blew up with support and love. They were talking about my comeback on sports talk radio and the evening news, and fans on the street were being interviewed about whether I could make it back or not.

Why did this touch such a nerve? Pittsburgh, man. Remember, this is a city that once wrapped its collective arms around a Vietnam vet with a blown-off foot; all Rocky Bleier did was win the Bronze Star and Purple Heart on the battlefield and *then* defy all the odds to help lead the Steelers to four Super Bowl championships in the seventies. This town doesn't just pull for underdogs; it sees itself in them.

Now here I came, saying, *You can paralyze me, but even that ain't going to keep me down.* That grit? Man, that was *all* Burgh.

* * *

Trusting the process meant embracing the hard, slow tedium of physical therapy. When I was out of the wheelchair, I could maybe take a shaky step or two with my right foot; my left side still wasn't totally firing.

But early in my stay at Mercy, I received a wonderful gift from my godmother, Robina, another of my true believers. It was a bracelet that said *"Walking Miracle."* Talk about signs. Shortly after I put that bracelet on, the PTs put my legs in braces attached to a walker, and—what do you know?—I was *walking*. Now, do I think that bracelet was somehow magic? Nah. But I think it was one of many important symbols of the power of belief and faith and prayer.

Most mornings at Mercy, I'd be transported back over to UPMC for a couple of hours in a hyperbaric chamber.

Remember how Dr. O said they were going to try *everything* in my treatment? Hyperbaric oxygen treatment, or HBOT, fell under that. The goal is to increase the body's absorption of oxygen in order to promote healing. During HBOT, I'd lie down in a tubelike chamber for two hours and breathe while the air pressure was gradually increased until it was two to three times greater than normal. Usually, the oxygen we breathe in gets absorbed by the lungs and distributed to our tissues and organs by the heart and blood vessels. HBOT allows oxygen to be dissolved in the blood, body fluids, bone tissue, lymph nodes, and— critical for me—cerebral spinal fluid, which surrounds the brain and spinal column. Oxygen-rich fluids then travel to areas where blood circulation is clogged or blocked.

The lower part of my body was waking up, but it

was still an uneven process; HBOT could help speed up my recovery. For example, I could take tentative, shaky steps, but I still didn't have much control over my feet, particularly on my left side.

After the hyperbaric chamber, I'd head back over to Mercy for PT. At the beginning, we'd do exercises that worked on my balance, on standing up, on getting sensation back in areas—like my left foot—that still weren't firing yet.

I'd get on the same type of stationary bike Christopher Reeve used to use. My legs and feet would be strapped in and electrodes would trigger muscles in my thighs and butt to contract and relax. Using handlebars, my arms could help my legs power the cycling. Not only was this a workout, but, I was told, studies showed that patients who had incomplete neurological function from the waist down saw, on average, a 25 percent increase in oxygen intake and a 37 percent jump in heart rate. And it was also a reminder to my body of a familiar physical activity. We were retraining my muscle memory.

With each passing day, I could feel different parts of my body waking up. Within a week, I was snugly attached to a treadmill and walking on it. The toe exercises I'd been doing every day had brought back some control.

But then, I was going above and beyond the PTs' protocol: after all this work in the morning, Jerome would stop by every afternoon and we'd give the folks at Mercy a glimpse of what an athlete's work-out looks like. He'd bring some dumbbell weights and we'd go to town on my upper body and core. Jerome would spot me as I hung on the parallel bars, pulling myself up time and again, until my arms were too tired for another rep. Then there was the TRX row, a back-strengthening exercise where I'd pull my body forward while holding on to straps attached diagonally to an overhead pull-up bar.

Jerome was a beast. By then he'd opened his own spot in Pittsburgh, Dynamic Performance Development, but any business interests took a backseat to Team Shazier. When I got hurt, Jerome was one of the first at my bedside, clutching my hand. "We're going to get through this," he said. "I'm here for you, and I love you. You're my brother."

The best trainers know they're not just in the body-building business; they're really in the *spirit* building business. Jerome was as much a motivator and coach as he was a trainer. He made me want to get better, and he kept reminding me of the bigger picture. "Even when it's looking bad, God is still good," he liked to say, particularly when I was reaching exhaustion on a set of reps.

Soon I was ready to get on home. I'd continue my rehab at Mercy as an outpatient, and Jerome and I would meet up every day at the gym, too. Before my official discharge on February 1, I had a visitor: "Big Ben" Roethlisberger stopped by—wearing camo shorts on a cold Burgh day—and we had some laughs. I posted a photo of us together with wide smiles on Instagram with this message:

I've had a lot of 1st downs at UPMC, but you know being the defensive guy I am, my mind is on 3 and out. With that being said, I want everyone to know that I'm moving on to the next step of the process. Today's a big day for me as I'm officially being released from the hospital.

I want to take a moment to thank the people who have helped me the past two months. First and foremost, I want to thank God because at the end of the day I don't think I'd be making progress without His vision and hands protecting me and my family. I will continue to trust in Him and thank Him, because it all starts with Him.

To my family: you've been my rock. Words can't express how thankful I am for you Michelle, RJ, Mom, Dad, and VJ for always being there for me. You're my everything.

To Jerome: my trainer and best friend. Thank you for being there from day 1 and every day after continuing to push me to be better every day....

The support from my teammates has been truly amazing. From former players to current players and their families—they have helped me and my family day to day with visits and gifts. We can't thank you enough.

I want to thank Mr. Rooney, Coach T, Mr. Colbert,

and the entire Steelers organization for the unwavering support they've given me. I knew they were an amazing organization, but more than ever they're family to me....

I want everyone to know that all of the support and prayers are absolutely being answered. I will continue to work hard and push and find a way back. #Shalieve #Steelers #prayfor50

* * *

It's hard to think of a better string of good fortune than that which the Steelers' chairman, Dan Rooney, experienced in late 2008 and early 2009. Not only did his team win its sixth Super Bowl, beating the Cardinals, but Rooney's candidate for president, Barack Obama, made history by becoming the forty-fourth president of the United States. Rooney was a major donor to Obama, and on St. Patrick's Day 2009 the president showed his appreciation by appointing Rooney to the position of ambassador to Ireland.

Rooney had already turned the day-to-day running of the Steelers over to his son Art Rooney II, and his appointment was the culmination of a lifetime commitment to the Irish peace movement. His Irish roots ran deep, and his love for Ireland was reciprocated, as evidenced by the Steelers bar in Belfast that still rocks on game day.

In Pittsburgh in 1976, Rooney had cofounded the Ireland Funds, a fundraising network that supports Irish peace and culture. I was invited to an Ireland Funds dinner honoring the legacy of Mr. Rooney shortly after I came home from Mercy, and it was at that dinner that the seeds of a pretty cool idea were planted.

Both Kevin Colbert and Coach Tomlin had said to me, in a kind of offhanded, joking way on a couple of occasions, that I ought to attend the upcoming NFL Draft and announce the team's first-round pick. I shrugged it off. I mean, I still wasn't confidently taking more than a couple of steps. I wasn't ready to appear before the world live on ESPN.

Well, apparently the idea was more than an offhanded joke. NFL commissioner Roger Goodell was at the Ireland Funds dinner, and he put his arm around me. "I just love the idea of you appearing with me onstage at the draft!" he said. Uh-oh.

I told Mr. Goodell that I didn't know if I could do it but I'd keep him apprised of my progress. No doubt Colbert and Tomlin liked the idea because it would make for great public relations—a moving, newsworthy moment. But I suspected they were up to something else, too.

They were both coaches, and, as such, they both challenged me time and again throughout my rehab— just as if I were still an active roster player. Jerome and I started doing our workouts at the team's UPMC

Rooney Sports Complex, which in itself said something about their commitment to my comeback: most
teams don't allow individual players' trainers in their
facilities. Remember, Tom Brady and the Patriots once
clashed when he wanted his guy, Alex Guerrero, with
him in the building. Teams' strength and conditioning
coaches don't want outsiders on their turf, potentially
second-guessing their coaching. I can understand
that—too many voices can mess with a player's
mindset.

But Colbert and Tomlin had seen how good Jerome
was and how much I needed him. So there we'd be,
me and Jerome, doing our thing, and almost every
day either Colbert or Tomlin would peek in and
push me. "You can do more reps than that!" Colbert
might yell.

God forbid I'd miss a day. "Where were you yester-
day?!" Tomlin would snap.

It was good-natured ball busting, sure, but sometimes that's what coaching is. They were always
pushing me, which in turn gave me confidence. *They
must think I have a good shot at coming back.*

Now they'd provided me with my greatest challenge yet: walking in front of the world at the draft.
I was nervous as heck. The plan was that Michelle
and I would walk together to the podium, where I'd
announce the Steelers' pick. Before the draft, Michelle
and I spent some time with her family in San Antonio,
where every day we'd practice walking together.

Don't get me wrong—I *could* walk, I knew that. But my left leg still dragged behind, I still wasn't steady on my feet, and I didn't know if I had the confidence to walk the whole distance from backstage to the podium and back. I'd been starting to have more of a public profile, like at the Ireland Funds dinner. I had recently posted a video on Instagram of myself doing pull-ups in the gym, and it had gone viral.

When I attended a Pittsburgh Penguins game, the fan-o-vision found me and I stood up to salute the crowd, which broke into a long standing ovation. "I've had the opportunity to meet him a couple times, and regardless of his situation, he's always got a smile on his face and a great attitude," Penguins stud Sidney Crosby said about me after that game. "And that's so important. It's so fun to be around people like that. It's contagious. I think he's a great example to everybody."

But this was different; this was *walking*, not just standing, and millions of eyes would be on me. But not doing it? That was never an option. In addition to practicing with Michelle, I had to do a whole lot of distanced self-talk, reminding myself of what Aurelius had said: "It is not death that a man should fear, but he should fear never beginning to live."

I knew I'd regret it if I gave into my fears, and the Stoics convinced me that Colbert, Tomlin, and Goodell had conspired to provide me with an opportunity. "The greater the difficulty, the more glory in surmounting it," Epictetus wrote. "Skillful pilots gain their reputation from storms and tempests."

So it was that on the night of April 26, 2018, Michelle, R.J., and I found ourselves backstage at AT&T Stadium in Arlington, Texas, waiting for Commissioner Goodell to introduce me prior to the Steelers' first-round pick, fifteenth overall.

"We have a very special moment," the commissioner said. "To make the announcement of the Pittsburgh Steelers selection, we are honored to have with us an extraordinary man who continues to amaze us with his unyielding determination and his unwavering spirit. We are so proud of him, and he inspires us all. Please welcome, joined by his fiancée, Michelle, Ryan Shazier."

Out we came. I couldn't hear the applause; if you watch a clip of the draft today, you can see that my face was frozen in concentration. I was focusing on the twenty-eight steps it would take to get me to that podium.

I was wearing a black shirt and sequined blazer, clutching Michelle's hand, walking unsteadily with more than a limp—really, a pretty pronounced hitch in my left side's gait. At the microphone, I announced the Steelers' choice of defensive back Terrell Edmunds of Virginia Tech. When Edmunds reached the stage, we embraced and then posed for photos.

R.J. came onstage, and I noticed a tear dripping down Michelle's cheek. In the audience, right up front, was a pack of Steelers fans, all crying and hugging one another.

On ESPN, a Twitter post from Odell Beckham Jr. filled the screen—*"God is so good @RyanShazier i love you brother"*—and when the ESPN studio crew went to Deion Sanders for the post-pick interview with Edmunds, he was all choked up. "That just tore me apart, guys," Deion said. "I apologize. I'm trying to be professional, but that got me."

There were a few seconds of dead air—which can feel like a lifetime on live TV—and then Deion continued. "God," he said. "Praying for that gentleman."

It became a widely seen moment, and in the days that followed I heard so many opinions about what my walking at the draft meant. I heard that it was a testament to God's grace. That it was a symbol of how brutal and unforgiving football could be. That it was inspiring. That it was sad. That it showed what prayer and hard work could do.

I guess it was all those things. To me, it was neither triumph or tragedy. It was another part of the journey.

* * *

Back at home, Michelle had requested a house call from Dr. O. We'd grown to be friends with him, so this was not that unusual. But Michelle's agenda was.

We sat with him in our living room. I began by telling Dr. O, kind of matter-of-factly, that since I'd last seen him, I'd regained total control of my bladder. His eyes widened.

"That's huge, guys," he said. "You should consider that a big first down." He went on to explain that, in his experience, patients don't rank walking again as their number one goal. Regaining control of their bladder, so they don't have to catheterize six times a day, is the most desired hurdle to get over among those with spinal injuries. That's followed by, in order, regaining sex function and overcoming neuropathic pain syndrome, a shooting or burning sensation that can come and go. Only after those three concerns are addressed does the typical spinal cord injury patient rank walking again as a top goal.

"Most patients will be okay with a life in a wheel-chair if they don't have to deal with the other three conditions," Dr. O said.

At this, Michelle looked kind of sheepish. Because our sex life was...confusing. On a few occasions, the equipment seemed to work. But there was no rhyme or reason to it. We didn't know what was going on down there.

"As you know, we're getting married," Michelle said. "Is having a baby out of the question for us?"

This is why you gotta love Dr. O, because his response wasn't what you might expect from a physician. He looked at me and started to giggle. "I have great news for you, my man," he said. "That thing is going to work for you. Not only will you guys be able to have sex, but you'll be able to conceive—the old-fashioned way!"

Dr. O studied our faces for a long second. "I think you both just gave off a sigh of relief, for two completely different reasons!" he said. We were all laughing now.

Later, we hugged and called our parents. When I told mine what the doctor had said, Dad, as usual, had some wisdom for the moment. He reminded me that there was plenty of journey left to travel, and that the road map to it was in my own story.

"Don't forget, son," he said, "everything you've been through has prepared you for everything you're facing. From college to the pros, you've been tested and you've learned and grown. Think about that. Nothing's ever easy. The lessons are all right there for you."

CHAPTER SEVEN

DAVID WITH THE SLINGSHOT

If you've never been to an Ohio State Buckeye game at the Shoe—Ohio Stadium's nickname because of its horseshoe shape—you've missed a great fan experience. And as a player, there's no better place to play.

I still get chills when I think about running out there with 105,000 fans chanting "O-H-I-O" in a deafening loop for ten minutes leading up to kickoff. Your heart beats so fast you have to run in place on the sidelines just to make sure your legs will work when called upon.

At Ohio State, football is a religion. Sure, a lot of schools say that. But trust me: there is nothing like Buckeye Nation. A few years ago, FanSided 250, which ranks fan bases, named Ohio State fans the best not just in the nation but in the *world*. The year after I left, the *New York Times* published an interactive map charting the college football fandom in every county in the country, based on Facebook likes, and it showed that Ohio State traveled better than any other school. How else to explain why the Buckeyes are the second-most-popular team in places like Maricopa County, Arizona, and Clark County, Las Vegas?

The Buckeyes of Columbus are a deeply encoded part of the state's DNA, which explains the slogan that so often unites the fan base: *"Ohio State versus the World."* Playing for Ohio State was an amazing experience; not only was my team my extended family, but so was the whole state.

And to think, initially, I didn't even want to go there. I was from Florida, man. Why in the world would I want to go north, where it's, like, *cold*?

* * *

In my senior year of high school, my last period of the day was kind of a freebie. I'd sit in the computer lab and mess around. One day, late in the 2010 term, my classmate Jeremy Cash came in grinning from ear to ear.

"Ryan, check out the internet," he said. "Coach Meyer just retired."

Jeremy knew I'd already committed to the University of Florida and its head coach, Urban Meyer. "What are you talking about? Coach Meyer didn't retire; I just talked to him last week," I said.

But there was the headline. He was stepping down

because of health issues. *This can't be happening*, I thought. Growing up, I'd always wanted to play for Florida State, but when it came time for me to choose a college, Florida's Coach Meyer made all the difference. When I was being recruited, other coaches tried to sell me on what would be in it for *me* if I attended their school—how much playing time I'd get, what the tricked-out accommodations in the athletes' dorm were like. But Coach Meyer, intense and calm, talked about building a *culture* of winning. I could become better under him. After committing to Florida, I realized I hadn't taken advantage of any recruiting trips. So, just a couple of weeks ago, I'd spoken to Coach Meyer to ask what seemed now to be a pretty naive question.

"Coach, I'm committed to Florida and everything, but I've barely been out of state, so I was wondering if it would be okay with you if I just visit some other schools," I'd said.

Of course, Coach Meyer had responded as any coach would. "You're committed here," he'd said. "We really don't want you visiting any other schools."

Okay, I'd understood, and I'd reiterated that I'd honor my commitment. That conversation had been, maybe, ten days ago. Now *he was* leaving? At first, I felt betrayed. But after Florida's loss to Alabama in the SEC Championship Game, Coach Meyer had checked himself into the hospital to be treated for dehydration. In consultation with his doctors, he was stepping down to get healthy and put his family first. How could I knock him for that?

Within a matter of days, assistant coaches for both Louisiana State University and Ohio State were in my high school coach's office, both with offers to visit their campuses as soon as possible. I loved my trip to LSU. I clicked with the guys on the team I hung out with. When I called my dad from Louisiana, I said, "I think this is the place for me," but he put the brakes on: "I hear what you're saying, but whatever you do, don't commit until you see the other place and we can talk it over."

I'm glad he said that, because the LSU coaches put on a hard sell to get me to commit then and there. The next day, I was in Columbus, where it was ten degrees outside. The students were on break, so the campus was empty in addition to being in a deep freeze. It wasn't looking good for the Buckeyes.

Back home, I told Dad about the dudes on the team at LSU. "I had fun because of the people I was hanging out with," I said. "They reminded me of the type of person that I am."

Dad got that, but his job was to be practical and make sure I was seeing the big picture. Ohio State had a huge alumni base, so if the NFL didn't work out, that could be a huge plus for my future. Plus, Ohio State and its defensive coach, Luke Fickell, had a knack for sending linebackers on to the NFL. Not only that, head coach Jim Tressel was recognized nationwide as a top-notch coach. "And if you do make it to the NFL, you'll have experience playing in the cold at Ohio State," Dad said.

Dad also laid out the downside. He explained that going to Ohio State meant I'd be far from home—far enough that he and Mom wouldn't be able to jump in the car and visit. "You'll be all alone there, Ryan," he said. But the thing that tipped the scales in Ohio State's favor was pretty atypical.

I knew there'd be a senior ahead of me on the roster, which meant I wouldn't get much playing time as a freshman. Most recruits are looking for assurances that they'll start from day one. But, remember, I'd played defensive end in high school. I needed to learn how to be a linebacker. I thought this could be an opportunity for me to be a sponge and really improve.

So Ohio State it was. But the drama wasn't over.

Head coach Jim Tressel's nickname was "the Senator," owing to his stately bearing, his high-mindedness, and his politician-like skill at spinning answers to questions. He was a legend, so it was shocking when, in May 2011, his ten years at the helm of Ohio State blew up in scandal.

An investigation had begun when six players—including star quarterback Terrelle Pryor—were found to have been selling Buckeye memorabilia to a tattoo parlor owner in violation of NCAA rules. Turned out, Coach Tressel had known about the sales long before the investigation and hadn't reported them. When other accusations surfaced—like the questionable sale of cars from local dealerships to Buckeye players—Tressel's fate was sealed. He resigned.

So before a single snap of my collegiate career, I'd committed to two teams whose coaches had both stepped down. What a way to start out. Coach Fickell, who I loved, would serve as interim head coach. But the Ohio State program was in total disarray, and I had to figure out how to make it work for me.

* * *

You know what's an amazing feeling? When you're David and you've got the slingshot. That's how I felt. Like: *You may think you know, but you got another thing coming.*

It was late in my freshman season. The previous week, Andrew Sweat, the senior linebacker I was understudying, had gone down with a bad concussion. (Andrew—an academic All-American—would go on to sign as an undrafted free agent with the Cleveland Browns. But then he'd have a change of heart and retire from the game because of his concussions. Law school seemed like a safer bet to him.)

Mom and Dad were back in Florida, watching the game at a local sports bar. They met a woman visiting from Ohio at the bar and started talking. She was a Buckeyes fan. They told her their son was on the team but had hardly been playing.

"Is that your son?" she said. "Number ten?"

"Well, I'll be," Dad said. "There he is."

With Andrew out hurt, I'd been called into action and made seven tackles with one sack in an overtime loss at Purdue. This woman and my mom and dad had one fine time celebrating together. They became fast friends, and Robina, who had no kids of her own, became my godmother. When she got back to Columbus after her Florida vacation, she cooked me some fine homemade meals. Later, she'd give me that *"Walking Miracle"* bracelet. She's a godsend.

After my coming-out party against Purdue, I was making my first start against an iconic college football program: Penn State. They were in the middle of their own scandal—involving pedophilia charges against former assistant coach Jerry Sandusky—but they were still a formidable opponent on the field.

That's when I felt it: *ready.* I was ready. I was a freshman in his first start. Everyone knew what that meant: I'd have a target on my back the whole game. My coaches had prepared me well from an x's-and-o's standpoint, but the real key was my mental outlook: Would I shrink? Or did I welcome the challenge?

I loved the feeling I had in the game's opening minutes. *David with the slingshot.* Knowing that those dudes on the other side of the ball were looking to attack me and that I had the power to do something about that. This was an opportunity. Looking across the line of scrimmage at those Nittany Lions in their plain black-and-white uniforms, I thought: *Bring it.*

I'm either going to prove you wrong or prove you right. Either way, it's up to me.

That first quarter, even I was surprised by how quick I was to the ball. There I was out in the flat, breaking up a screen. Sidestepping a block on an end run to take down a runner for a loss. Hitting the tight end over the middle so hard his mama felt it. Five tackles in the opening fifteen minutes. Later, I stopped Penn State quarterback Matt McGloin at the goal line.

I could feel my confidence growing with each play, but I wasn't going to show it by talking trash. I've never done that. When I was little, my mom never let me crack jokes at other people's expense, and I've always felt that the guys who talk trash are just like the kids I grew up with who would tease other kids to try to embarrass or upset them. The type of kids who would make fun of my bald head.

So each time I made a play, there was no dance, no commentary, no finger-pointing. We ended up losing a hard-fought game 20–14, but I'd proven myself by making fifteen tackles and, more importantly, by being in the right position on every single play.

Afterward, the hoopla felt a little surreal until I talked to Dad. "If I can make fifteen tackles as a freshman in my first start," I told him, "maybe I *can* play in the NFL."

Dad was thinking the same thing. He'd already given me some great advice before the game: "Stay tight with your team's strength coach." You spend more time in the weight room than you do at practice, he'd explained. Your strength coach is feeding your head coach information about you—so it's up to you to control that. Do you want him reporting back that Shazier is a complainer? That Shazier is one of those guys you have to tell more than once to do something? Or do you want your coach to know how coachable you are and that you'll do anything to get better?

After the Penn State game, Dad and I spoke again. I was just starting college and I loved Ohio State. But now we had new information. My dream had always been to play in the NFL. "We want you to ultimately get your degree, but also to follow your dreams," Dad said, speaking for Mom, too.

So, although I didn't tell my teammates or coaches, after talking it over with Dad, I made a promise to myself. I'd consider myself committed to the Buckeyes for one thousand days, which would take me just through my junior year. At that point, if the NFL scouts believed I could be drafted in the first three rounds, I'd leave for the league.

That ambitious goal only fueled my fire to succeed even more. Our season went south: we finished at 6–7. But after I was inserted into the starting lineup for our last three games, I led the team with thirty-three tackles. Ohio State decided not to bring back Coach Fickell. And you'll never believe who they hired.

* * *

"I guess I was just destined to coach you," Urban Meyer told me after it was announced that he'd come out of his yearlong retirement to be the new coach for Ohio State.

"That's crazy, Coach," I agreed, laughing. "I guess *I* was meant to play for *you.*"

It all made sense, though. Coach Meyer was as much an Ohioan as anyone could be. He was born in Toledo to parents who'd met in Cincinnati. He was raised in Ashtabula in the state's northeast corner, home to wineries and covered bridges. He graduated from the University of Cincinnati and Ohio State. At the start of his coaching career, Coach Meyer's dream was to someday be an *assistant* coach at Ohio State.

This was a homecoming for him. But three weeks after he was hired, the NCAA levied sanctions against the program for its past abuses under Coach Tressel: a postseason ban and scholarship reductions.

No one had seen it coming, but Coach Meyer didn't let it distract him from his goal of changing our team culture. After the sanctions were announced, he called a team meeting—for 6 a.m. Some guys came late, others didn't show at all. So he called another meeting for the next day—also at 6 a.m. He had strength coach Mickey Marotti start us on frigid outdoor early-morning workouts. I was among those bitching about them, until I realized we were all growing closer as a team. Coach Meyer had a psychology degree, and he was always messing with your mind. He knew that if we all shared in basic training–like misery, we'd bond into a unit.

Sure enough, that's what we did. No one expected us to dominate in my sophomore season, but we were on a mission, and so was I. I'd work out before practice and watch film afterward. It was a breakout season for me; against Penn State, I had eight tackles, two sacks, and an interception that I ran back for the game-winning touchdown. But the game I remember the most—sort of—came late in the season at Madison, Wisconsin.

We rolled in with a 10–0 record, and we'd be facing the Badgers running back Montee Ball, who was a touchdown away from breaking the career college football scoring record. In the fourth quarter, up 14–7, I had a bead on Melvin Gordon on an end-around. Remember what Dad had always said? Tackle *through* the opponent. I accelerated and lowered my head and hit Melvin so hard that *I* got a concussion. I lay on the field in the fetal position. While struggling to my feet, I was vaguely aware of a question being put to me:

"You all right?"

"Yeah, bruh," I said, slowly shaking my head.

"Bruh?" my questioner said, sounding surprised.

"I'm awright, bruh," I struggled to say. "No worries."

That's when I looked up, and the face of my interviewer

came into focus: Coach Meyer. Now, Coach Meyer is not a bruh. He's as straitlaced and intense as they come. But we've called each other "bruh" ever since.

This, of course, was before concussion protocols. Today, there's no way I'd be able to come back and play after a hit like that without undergoing a bunch of tests. Back then, I'd just had my bell rung. After a while on the sideline, I ran up to Coach. "I'm good to go, Coach," I said.

"You sure?" he asked, but I was already running onto the field.

Wisconsin was driving for what would be the game-tying score. It was fourth and one from the one-yard line with two minutes forty-six seconds left. I'd watched all that film of Montee Ball. I *knew* what was coming. Ball liked to hurdle the line and extend his arms with the ball out in front of him, trying to break the plane. I leaped over my down linemen *and* his offensive line to meet him head-on in the air at just the right moment, hitting him *and* popping the ball free at the point of impact. We recovered, denying Ball his record-setting touchdown, and went on to win in overtime. Of course, I only have vague memories of the game—and most of those, I think, are from watching it later.

I was already learning what success is really about: figuring stuff out. Problem-solving, I'd started to realize, is a skill. And even though we were undefeated at the time, there was a lot to overcome on an Urban

Meyer team. No doubt utilizing all he'd learned as an undergraduate psychology major, Coach seemed to be always waging psychological warfare on his players. I might have thought I'd just played a helluva game, but when the team was watching film of it the next day, he might stop the tape and say, "Look at how Ryan blew this assignment right here. He keeps doing that and he might not start." He was always encouraging competition among teammates.

At times, you'd know you'd played great, but he wouldn't acknowledge it. Other times, when you knew you totally screwed up, he might say something encouraging. He had a way of keeping you on your toes at all times.

Not every player could withstand the pressure of playing for Coach Meyer, of meeting his standards, of always looking over your shoulder and wondering if that dude at the next locker was better than you and about to take your job. But I loved it, because it motivated me. When he called me out or withheld praise, I felt like Coach was challenging me to prove him wrong. It drove me to want to get better every day, to be the first at practice and the last to leave, to hit harder and run faster than anyone on the field.

I started every game of my sophomore year and placed second in the Big Ten with 115 tackles, including a league-high 17 for losses. Five sacks, three forced fumbles. Sounds amazing, right? What neither watching the game nor reading the stats tell you is what I had to overcome in order to tell that story. There's *always* something to overcome.

What only my teammates knew was that I barely practiced the whole second half of the season. I had a hernia, and it got so bad that some weeks, I could only participate in Friday's walk-through. So I had to figure out a way to prepare all week for Saturday without actually practicing. Sure, that involved watching film and visualizing plays in great detail. But was there a way I could sort of *virtually* practice? Could I be out there on the field with my guys, participating in practice, without doing the movements and pivots that would fire up my groin?

That's when I started doing mental reps. I'd line up in the rear of the practice, with no pads on, some forty yards behind the play. That way, I could see the play without running the risk of being *in* the play. Once the offense snapped the ball, I'd read the play and react, careful not to take any false steps. If it was a running play to the right, I'd shuffle right—right, left, right—concentrating on getting the perfect jump at the most advantageous angle. Maybe I took five steps total rather than thirty. If it was a pass, I'd likewise read the quarterback while backpedaling five steps before breaking toward the play. In each case, I was working on conditioning myself to react and committing to memory—and muscle memory—what I'd do in response to everything that week's opposing offense might have up its sleeve.

In our season finale, I had five tackles and a sack, and Braxton Miller, our star quarterback, rushed for 108 yards and threw for 189 more. We beat Michigan, 26–21, to finish an undefeated season at 12–0, though we were banned from Bowl competition.

But that was why Urban Meyer was such a great coach. Being undefeated wasn't good enough. He knew that we weren't yet competitive with the likes of Alabama, which went on to win the national championship by destroying Notre Dame 42–14 in the Bowl Championship Final.

Almost before that game had even ended, we started receiving texts from Coach Meyer: *"The Chase is on. The Chase is real."*

The chase to reach the Crimson Tide's level became his rallying cry. Within days, signs proclaiming "The Chase" were plastered around campus and our team's facility. It would take two years to complete the chase, but, to a man, we were united in focusing on it.

The legendary management consultant and author Peter Drucker wrote that "culture eats strategy for breakfast," a point Coach Meyer instilled in us again and again. "Talent, schemes, tactics, and plans cannot replace a strong culture," Coach Meyer wrote in his 2015 book, *Above the Line: Lessons in Leadership and Life from a Championship Season.* "A great culture can make even a mediocre strategy successful, but a weak culture will undermine even the best strategy....Culture determines attitude and effort. Once strategy has been developed, success becomes a matter of attitude and effort. And that's where culture comes in."

How did Coach Meyer change the culture at Ohio State? By being intentional, down to the smallest detail. Relentless effort and competitive excellence were two of his touchstones, but so was the "power of the unit." Assistant coaches were dubbed "unit leaders," and they were charged with teaching trust and team cohesion throughout the locker room. Culture wasn't just some sayings painted on the wall; it was how you behaved, to and *for* one another. Our culture valued "ownership, accountability and responsibility," and we didn't accept "blame, excuses or denial."

Coach Meyer would even go on to develop a type of mathematical formula: E + R = O; Event plus Response equals Outcome. To Coach Meyer, we might not have control over every event, but we have total control over how we *respond* to each event. And, given that outcome is a combination of event *and* response, we were never powerless to affect the outcome, no matter the situation. I didn't know it at the time, but in remaking the Ohio State culture by emphasizing focus on what we *could* control, Coach Meyer was giving us a lesson in Stoicism.

* * *

Because of our undefeated 2012 season and our highly touted recruiting class, Ohio State football was ranked

Even at 10 years old, I was obsessed with earning football trophies on the field.

At one point in youth football, some parents complained to Dad: "Ryan tackles too hard."

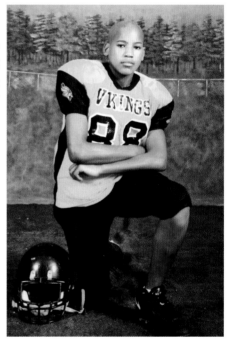

Dad, a pastor and football coach, with both sons: Vernon II (left) and a bald future NFL Pro Bowler

At Plantation High School, I was too quick for opposing offensive linemen and had 22 sacks my junior year.

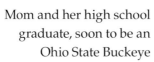

Mom and her high school graduate, soon to be an Ohio State Buckeye

Buckeye fans are the craziest, wildest in the nation. And our family became a Buckeye family.

In three seasons at Ohio State, I had 317 tackles in 39 games, including 15 sacks.

Nebraska running back Ameer Abdullah running into a Shazier buzzsaw

Coach Urban Meyer, pictured here with me and my teammate Jake Stoneburner, was a master motivator who led us to a streak of 24 straight wins.

At the NFL Combine, I opened some eyes with a 42-inch vertical and a 130-inch broad jump. On Ohio State's Pro Day, I ran a 4.36 forty-yard dash.

I had no inkling that the Pittsburgh Steelers were interested in me. But then my phone rang and it was Coach Mike Tomlin, welcoming me to the Burgh.

When NFL Commissioner Roger Goodell calls your name as a first round selection in the NFL Draft, you feel a range of emotions...especially *gratitude*.

A Steeler, going to war. *(Icon Sports Wire / Scott Terna via Getty Images)*

From 2016. That's a bad man. *(John Grieshop via Getty Images)*

"I can't move my legs." *(John Grieshop via Getty Images)*

Already plotting my comeback.

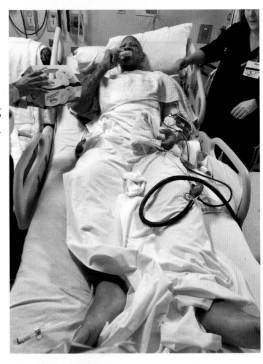

A week after my injury, my man Big Ben Roethlisberger carried my jersey off the field after our game against Baltimore at Heinz Field.

I still get choked up when I think about just how much Pittsburgh had my back. *(Icon Sportswire / Mark Alberti via Getty Images)*

Think we're only intense about football? Michelle and I lead the Penguins faithful in fandom. *(Icon Sportswire / Jeanine Leech via Getty Images)*

Left to right: Big Ben Roethlisberger, Coach Mike Tomlin, me, and Cam Heyward during the national anthem in a 2018 game. My brothers in arms. *(Icon Sportswire / Roy K. Miller via Getty Images)*

At the 2018 NFL Draft, after nearly five months of rehab, Michelle and I walked the 28 steps to the podium to announce Pittsburgh's first round draft choice.

The family Shazier, decked out on our emotional wedding day.

second in the major college football polls as the 2013 season got underway. And we lived up to the hype.

We opened conference play with wins over Wisconsin (31–24) and Northwestern (40–30), both nationally ranked. As the season wore on, we got more efficient at putting teams to sleep early. Penn State? A 63–14 romp. Purdue? 56–0. Illinois? 60–35. In that game, I earned Big Ten Player of the Week honors with 16 tackles and 3.5 tackles for loss. The next week, I outdid that.

Indiana had one of the highest-scoring offenses in the country, but we shut them down. I had twenty tackles, including sixteen solo stops, plus five tackles for loss, a forced fumble, a sack, and a pass breakup in a 42–14 win. That tied the school record for total tackles and tackles for loss. I was the first Buckeye to record twenty tackles since A. J. Hawk in 2004 and the first to have sixteen solo tackles since Tom Cousineau in 1978.

We won a nail-biter in Ann Arbor, barely beating archrival Michigan 42–41 when my teammate Tyvis Powell picked off the Wolverines' two-point conversion pass attempt for the win in the end zone with thirty-two seconds left. Phew, that was a close one.

But something happened to us after that game. We'd been on a mission all season, and we entered the Big Ten Championship Game against Michigan State with a 12–0 record. Not only that, but we hadn't lost in twenty-four games. Knowing that Alabama had already lost to Auburn, we entered the Big Ten Championship Game knowing that a win would have us playing for the national title.

I don't want to say we overlooked Michigan State, but I think we fell into the trap of thinking ahead. Early in the game, our star cornerback, Bradley Roby, got hurt, so that didn't help. And we allowed Michigan State to get off to a fast start; before we knew it, we were down 17–0.

But the real problem was more psychological, and really rare for an Urban Meyer team. We had taken our eyes off the immediate task at hand; in our minds, we were already playing for the national title. But no one had clued Michigan State into that. We battled back, but it wasn't enough, and we lost, 34–24.

A few days before the game, I'd received my draft projection from the NFL. Typically, the league shares with highly touted players an average ranking that indicates how its scouts are thinking about them. Mine showed that I was likely a late first-round or early second-round pick. The worst-case scenario was that I'd drop to the late second or early third round.

Coach Meyer had a monster squad coming back for what would be my senior season. I knew that, if I stayed, I just might win a national championship. But now that I had a sense of where I'd be picked in the draft, I could taste the dream. Did I really want to risk getting hurt in my senior season now that I'd come so far?

"I'm leaving," I told Dad. After our loss to Michigan State, I went into Coach's office to let him know my plan. He was preoccupied with the preparations for our upcoming game against Clemson in the Orange Bowl. "Why don't we talk about this after the Orange Bowl?" he said.

Our game against Dabo Swinney's Clemson Tigers in the Orange Bowl was a good old-fashioned shoot-out. Both teams combined for more than a thousand yards; we were ahead 29–20 late in the third quarter, but we couldn't hold on. Our quarterback, Braxton Miller, was beat up and not at full strength. We had nothing left to give late in the game, and we lost in an upset, 40–35. We finished the season 12–2.

Looking back on it, I think we were all still stunned by the Michigan State loss. We had been so stoked to play for the national title. When we ended up not playing in that high-stakes game, there was a letdown. We all played hard, but mentally we had one foot in and one foot out. If I'm being honest, that's also a fair description of where my head was at in the game against Clemson. Once the ball was snapped, I played hard—but part of me was already in the NFL.

After the Orange Bowl game, Coach Meyer said something to me about sitting down back in Ohio to talk about my future.

"Coach, I love you, and I'll always be there for you," I told him. "But I've already made the decision to leave for the NFL." How far gone was I? Since the Orange

Bowl was in Florida, before leaving for the game I'd packed up all my stuff at school and had it shipped home to Fort Lauderdale. After the game, when the rest of the team boarded the plane back to Columbus, I stayed behind, ready to start my new life.

Sure, Ohio State would go on to win the national title the next season, which would have been my senior year. But my junior season was one of the best in the country. I was voted a first-team All-American by the Associated Press, *USA Today*, ESPN and *Sports Illustrated*. My 143 tackles led the Big Ten; I had six sacks and four forced fumbles.

I ain't gonna lie. I was pissed off when I got beat out for Big Ten Defensive Player of the Year by Wisconsin's Chris Borland. Don't get me wrong; Borland was a great player, with 102 tackles, 8.5 tackles for loss, four sacks, one forced fumble, and one fumble recovery. I just thought I'd had the more dominating year.

Did Borland get the honor because he was a senior? Who knows? And, in the end, who cares? All that mattered to me was that I was on to the next adventure. The next challenge. The thing I'd dreamed about since I was five years old. The NFL.

* * *

At the pre-draft NFL Scouting Combine, I opened some eyes with a 42-inch vertical, a 130-inch broad jump, and a 6.91-second three-cone drill. I turned more heads at Ohio State's Pro Day—when NFL scouts come to campus to put you through drills—with a 4.36 forty-yard dash. Now, *no one* expected a 4.36 forty out of me. That's the kind of number a wide receiver or running back might post. I don't know how it happened, but I just *flew*. That got some people talking right away. (Taken just two spots after me in the draft by Baltimore, C.J. Mosley posted a 4.63 forty.)

Draft night was at Radio City Music Hall in New York. As the fifteenth pick approached, the Dallas Cowboys were on the phone with my agent, telling him they'd be picking me with the sixteenth pick. Suddenly, *my* phone rang: a 412 area code. It was Mike Tomlin, the Steelers coach.

"Ryan, I want to welcome you to the Pittsburgh Steelers," he said. I was taken aback—no one had told me that the Steelers had any interest in me.

Coach Tomlin must have sensed my surprise. He explained that his team had other needs, but they couldn't pass me by because of my speed. God bless that Pro Day forty-yard dash. When he spoke to the press, Coach Tomlin described me as "splash-play capable." I'd never heard that phrase, but I'd soon come to find out that Coach Tomlin was full of phrases no one had heard before. But I knew what he was getting at: I was a playmaker.

I was the fifteenth pick of the NFL Draft, and I'd soon sign a four-year, $9 million deal, with a $5 million signing bonus. Dad and I had worked so hard for this.

His football dream had been taken from him in his teenage years, and all my life he'd guided me toward this moment. I hugged him and Mom, thanked them for all their sacrifices and support, and, grinning from ear to ear, pulled a Steelers jersey on over my suit before giving a series of interviews.

It was amazing and cool, but none of the stories that were written the next day told the *real* story of how I got to the NFL. The real story was in all those hours of film I watched, all those mental reps every day at practice my sophomore year, all those talks with my dad about how every play is an opportunity to do something positive for you and your team-mates, all those times Coach Meyer said something that fueled my drive to excel, and all that self-talk that convinced me I really was the best linebacker in the nation. When you watch a game, you see the finished product; you never really get a glimpse of just what went into getting there. The actual work *never* makes the highlight reel.

CHAPTER EIGHT

LUCK IS THE RESIDUE OF DESIGN

Ever since I was a little boy I'd been trained *not* to think on the football field. Football is all about being in the zone—that feeling where you're on autopilot and, because you've done the work of training your muscle memory, your conscious self gets out of your way and you just...go with the flow. You let your training take over.

Well, it was a bit of a rude awakening when, in the Steelers' spring OTAs (organized team activities) and then again in summer training camp, I found myself thinking for the first time ever about what I *should* have done after the whistle, rather than just doing it in real time.

Transitioning to the NFL, it turned out, was no easy task. The players were faster, stronger, and smarter than any I'd gone against before. I could no longer just rely on my speed.

It didn't help matters that Coach Tomlin and Keith Butler, our linebackers coach and soon to be our defensive coordinator, threw me into the fire. Unlike my freshman year at Ohio State, when I could watch and learn from Andrew Sweat, with the Steelers I was named the starting inside linebacker right from the get-go at the OTAs.

That didn't mean there weren't opportunities to learn—I just had to do it on the fly. Coach Butler was a real stickler and an absolute perfectionist. He had the chops to command respect, having started at linebacker for ten seasons with the Seattle Seahawks back in the day—he's still second on the club's all-time tackles list.

The Steelers had always fielded great linebackers— think back to the glory days of Jack Ham in the seventies. Coach Butler was keeping that tradition alive. Just two years prior, in 2012, his linebackers had been instrumental in making the Steelers the NFL's top-ranked defense, with five of them recording four or more sacks each, led by Pro Bowler Lawrence Timmons.

Butler had been instrumental in making my man James Harrison the monster he became on the field. James had been the 2008 NFL Defensive Player of the Year and earned five straight Pro Bowl selections under Butler's coaching. Harrison still holds the team record for sacks in a season, sixteen, in 2008.

Harrison had gone to Cincinnati for a year, but now

Colbert had brought him back, and, at thirty-six, he was still chugging along. (He'd go on to post 5.5 sacks in 2014.) Here, I knew instantly, was a teammate I could learn from.

Remember how, in college, Dad had taught me to pay attention to the impression I made on the team's strength coach, because he'd be reporting back to Coach Meyer? Well, now that same advice applied to Coach Butler. Normally there might be a good bit of distance between a positions coach and the head coach. But, as Dad was quick to point out, Coach Butler and Coach Tomlin went way back. They were on staff together at the University of Memphis in the 1990s—where Butler coached the linebackers, defensive line, and special teams, and Tomlin coached the defensive backs.

"When you're talking to Coach Butler, you're really talking to Coach Tomlin," Dad told me.

Coach Butler was a hard-ass coach. One mistake and he'd pull you from the game, even though, as players, we knew when we'd screwed up. Linebacker Sean Spence and I would laugh about it; we'd grown up not far from one another, and Sean had always been someone I looked up to. Our playbook was complicated, and when one of us would shoot the wrong gap or lapse into the wrong coverage set, we wouldn't even look toward the coaches. We knew our fate. Without breaking stride, we'd just make a bee-line for the sideline.

It was tough to get a rhythm going when you were being shuffled in and out like that, but Coach Butler's standards were just what I needed. I wanted to be held accountable on every play—how else could I get better? A lot of players bitched about how tough Coach Butler could be, but I think his standards really helped me make the tough adjustment to the NFL. What did Branch Rickey say? *"Luck is the residue of design."* Coach Butler might have been demanding, but I was learning from him. And he was reinforcing my own mania to *just. get. better. every. day.*

I still wasn't sure of myself on every play, but as my rookie season dawned, there I was—starting in the NFL. I'd have moments where everything would come together and I'd make the right read or a big play, and that would be enough to rekindle my confidence and keep my fire going. In golf, sports psychologists call it "intermittent reinforcement." No matter how unsure of yourself you might be, those one or two drives where you just *nail* it square and the ball lifts off like in your dreams is enough to keep you coming back, again and again, chasing perfection. Every day, I was getting a taste of what it *felt* like to play linebacker in the NFL, and it just made me hungrier.

In my first game, the home opener against Cleveland, I had six tackles, five of them solo, and I deflected a pass in a 30–27 win. The next week, in a 20–6 loss to the Ravens, I got more snaps—I must have made fewer mistakes—and ended up with fifteen tackles.

Okay, I thought, *I'm starting to get this.* I was learning that I couldn't gamble as much as I did in college, where I could backdoor each play with ease, time and again.

What do I mean by "backdoor"? Essentially, it's a defensive player's cutback. Imagine that it's a run play to the right. As a linebacker, I had to size up two things at the exact same time: I had to gauge how far the runner was behind his lead blocker, and I had to get a sense for how fast that lineman was coming toward me. If the lineman was close enough to me, I could foot-fake him, maybe throw in a head feint, and then backdoor the blocker by taking a quick step inside to make the play. Now, if the lineman was a step or two behind me, I could beat him to the outside and make the play that way. If we were both on the same path at the same angle, well, that meant that I had to take the blocker head-on and beat him in order to get to the runner.

In college, that third scenario rarely happened. As a matter of routine, I'd either backdoor the play or turn on the afterburners and beat my blocker outside. But in the pros, even linemen who were 330 pounds were too fast and too smart to fall for the same moves.

But, wouldn't you know it, just when I felt like I might be figuring this thing out... *setback.* In the first half of our third game at Carolina, I had six tackles. It felt like I was finally finding my groove. That's when, standing by a pile of bodies after a play had been whistled dead, my teammate Lawrence Timmons was blocked into me, undercutting my legs. I went down and knew instantly something was wrong. Hyperextended medial collateral ligament (MCL) in my knee. Out four weeks.

You just never know. In such a violent, fast-paced game, anything can happen to you, at any time. I mean, I was just standing there. Whistles had blown. And now my rookie season—did I tell you my goal had been to be the rookie defensive player of the year?—was in jeopardy. I made it back for two games, wins over Indianapolis and Baltimore, and then the freakiest thing happened.

Lightning can't strike twice, can it?

Think again, bruh.

Against Baltimore, in a game we'd win 43–23, I got hit *again* while just standing near a play, and I rolled my ankle. It was a high ankle sprain, a common injury that isn't serious but can take some time to heal. Ultimately, I'd miss *another* four weeks.

I knew there was some concern about my durability. I was seen as undersized—six foot one and 240 pounds put me on the smallish side for a linebacker. But these really were freak accidents. Coach Butler had my back by emphasizing my asset: speed. "Mobility is more important than girth," he told the press. "What you come to find out as a linebacker is you need the weight in the sense of the [blockers] you have to take on. But if you understand how to take people on in terms of technique, you need the mobility. You've got to be able to run to play this game."

While I was out, as at Ohio State, I lined up well behind my teammates during practice and ran through my mental reps. But things happen slower in practice than in real games—particularly in the NFL. Not getting game experience was definitely a setback.

Even as I struggled with injuries, things were looking up for the Steelers. They'd posted consecutive 8–8 seasons the last two years, but now, after our 27–24 win at Tennessee, we'd won four of our last five and our record stood at 7–4. After that game, I got a call when our charter flight landed in Pittsburgh at 1 a.m. Turned out, the NFL was just as hard to adjust to *off* the field.

* * *

All throughout my time at Ohio State, Tonika Knorwood and I had been close friends. One night, just before I went to the NFL Combine, Tonika and I got a little *too* friendly. One thing led to another. Stuff happens, right?

It had been a surprise when Tonika told me she was pregnant. Now, as our team flight landed back in Pittsburgh, she was calling at 1 a.m. "I think my water just broke," she said.

I had to get my bearings. It was only November 18. Our baby wasn't due for at least another month. But I guess Ryan Junior—R.J.—couldn't wait to meet us. I hopped in the car to make the three-hour drive from Pittsburgh to Columbus and got updates along the way. Tonika was heading into emergency surgery.

I wasn't exactly obeying the speed limit in the dead of night, but I still didn't get there in time. R.J. was born at 4:30 a.m., and his papa came sprinting into the hospital on a bum ankle ten minutes later. But when I laid eyes on that little guy, time stood still.

I'd known this moment was coming, of course, but I just kept mouthing the words to myself: *I have a son.* I'd spent so much time in church growing up, talking about blessings and grace. But I'd never *felt* as blessed and full of gratitude as I did that night, looking at my son.

I felt instantly changed. Here was somebody I'd kill or die for. Man, that type of instantaneous love is a powerful thing. I felt like I had a purpose now. And I felt a renewed sense of drive. Now I *had* to be a great football player, for this guy. Staring into R.J.'s eyes, I felt as if, in a matter of hours, *I'd* grown up.

Now, that didn't mean that, when I got back to Pittsburgh, I suddenly started living like a fifteen-year veteran of the league. No, I was young and suddenly rich and learning what life in the NFL was all about. A trio of defensive backs kind of took me under their wings. My man Will Allen was like a big brother to me. I was twenty-one years old and suddenly flush with cash for the first time in my life, and I'd be hanging at the club, spending way too much money.

"Little bro," Will would say, "you better save yourself some of that money. You're not going to remember where it all went."

It was great advice, and I should have listened more than I did. William Gay would be my wingman at the club and would always look out for me. But what I really took from Willie was what happened the mornings *after* we were out partying. No matter what had happened the night before, no matter how late we'd been out, no matter how our heads throbbed come daylight, there we'd be at 7 a.m., pumping iron in the weight room and then watching film together. It was a lesson in professionalism.

Will, Willie, and Mike Mitchell helped me out in one other way, too. All three were defensive backs. Just hanging with them, soaking up the game from their perspective, ultimately made me a much better defensive play-caller. Defensive captains often call plays that are convenient for them and their position, never stopping to think about how a certain call might expose a teammate. By listening to them, I started to get a feel for just how much stress cornerbacks are under. Later, when I was calling defensive plays, I'd be sensitive enough to audible out of a call that stretched one of them or made them vulnerable in single coverage. Will, Willie, and Mike helped me think about more than just myself, which made me a better teammate.

I came back to play the final three games of our

2014 season, all wins, over Atlanta, Kansas City, and Cincinnati, respectively. I had six tackles in the regular season finale against the Bengals, giving me thirty-six for the season in just eight games.

We finished 11–5, and there was much to be upbeat about. Our offense had been a thing of beauty. Ben Roethlisberger had had one of his best statistical years ever, with thirty-two touchdowns against only nine interceptions and a quarterback rating of 103.3. He had his pick of weapons on any given play. Markus Wheaton caught fifty-three passes after only six in his rookie year, and Martavis Bryant, after missing the team's first six games, caught eight touchdowns for over five hundred yards. And Le'Veon Bell had become a stud running back.

Then there was Antonio Brown, who was damn near unstoppable at wide receiver. He caught 129 balls for just shy of 1,700 yards and thirteen touchdowns. Good luck finding a more talented wideout. Antonio had a way of courting controversy in the media, but you had to love him as a game breaker on the field.

Defensively, we had good pieces, but we weren't always successful in getting them to fit together. Linebacker Lawrence Timmons was awesome, and defensive end Cam Heyward had 7.5 sacks. And my man William Gay had three interceptions *and* three touchdowns.

But when it was clutch time, we didn't come up with the big play often enough. In the playoffs, our offense was without Le'Veon Bell and Baltimore shut down Ben. We gave up thirty points to the Ravens and lost 30–17.

Someone once told me about the Japanese business philosophy of *kaizen*: the practice of continual improvement. If everyone in an organization is asking themselves every day "What can I do today to get better?" they're damn well going to be poised for success. They're changing and shaping their culture every day.

That's what it was like to be on a Mike Tomlin team. You had a locker room full of guys who were always pushing themselves. As a young player, I saw this and realized, *So that's how you get better.*

I knew I needed to do more. And that meant working my ass off.

* * *

Looking back on it now, the second game of our 2015 season was kind of my coming-out party. I'd shown flashes of potential in my rookie year, and in our season opener the week before, a 28–21 loss to Tom Terrific and the Patriots, I'd played solidly if unspectacularly, with seven tackles.

But I saw myself as a big-play guy, and I hadn't made any against Brady and the Pats. But that changed back home at Heinz Field against San Francisco. Our offense was clicking; Ben threw three touchdown passes and DeAngelo Williams rushed for three scores of his own in a 43–18 rout.

On defense, it felt like I knew where the ball was going before it went there. I had fifteen tackles, eleven of them solo. Not only was I first to the ball, but I was wrapping the ball carrier up before the cavalry arrived.

The 49ers quarterback was Colin Kaepernick, who was quick-footed and had a strong arm. His mobility didn't bother me, though. I loved the idea of matching my speed against anyone in the open field. When Kap tried to run up the middle, I was there to meet him. When he dumped the ball off into the flat, I was there to say, "Not today." In the third quarter, Kap faced a third and seven from his own twenty-one. I broke through the line on a blitz; sensing that I was coming for him, Kap turned and tried to scramble. But I didn't give him any angle for escape and dropped him for a seventeen-yard loss.

Now *that's* a big play, the kind that can deflate your opponent and change the momentum of a game. Sure enough, after we got the ball back, Ben hit Darrius Heyward-Bey to put us up 22–7. On the 49ers' next possession, running back Carlos Hyde—one of my Ohio State teammates—coughed up the ball and I pounced on it. We were on our way to a blowout win.

But how can we know the light without darkness? At one point, I hit wide receiver Quinton Patton so hard in the open field that I bruised my right shoulder—I thought it was nothing. Turned out, I'd sustained some nerve damage. Nothing to do but treat it in the PT room for a few weeks and wait for it to heal. Another injury. This time, though, the ache in my shoulder was a constant reminder of just how aggressively I'd played.

That was the message I heard loud and clear from Coach Tomlin after the 49ers game. In his postgame press conference, Coach Tomlin shook his head when asked about me. "He's that kind of player," he said—the kind of player who can change the tenor of a game, just as Dad had always preached.

When you watch football, you may think that turnovers are just mistakes. Someone "coughs up" the ball, or a quarterback throws an "errant" pass. Fumbles and interceptions appear to be just things that happen. How they affect the fortunes of a team seems to be mostly a matter of luck.

But whatever happened to luck being the residue of design? The legendary baseball man Branch Rickey is credited with coining that saying, but I know it also applies in football. The game only *looks* random and haphazard. The truth is, turnovers don't just happen. There is such a thing as turnover muscle memory, and I *work*ed at training mine all the time.

You hear coaches talk all the time about guys who they consider to be "big-play guys." At big moments, they come up big. On defense, that means you're a ball hawk. Coach Tomlin always said, "The reason we play football is for the ball." It sounds obvious, but trust me: it bears keeping top of mind that you can't score a touchdown without the ball. To me, the ball had always been the issue. My job was to figure out how to get it back. In a game, I didn't think to myself, *Let me tackle this guy.* I thought, *Let me get the ball.*

That was true in games—in big moments, I'd *tell* my teammates, "Let's get a fumble"—but it was also true in practice. I was always working on trying to get the ball.

In practice, it can be annoying to an offensive teammate when you're both out there without pads and you start trying to punch the ball free.

"Why you punchin' me, bro?" I was asked by more than one pissed-off teammate.

"Just trying to get better, bro," I'd say, and, as if I'd just reminded him that we're on the same team, we'd high-five.

In 2017, I welcomed T.J. Watt to our linebacking corps, and I marveled at how intensely he worked the turnover muscle. T.J. knew that if you didn't practice creating turnovers all the time in practice, forcing the ball out wouldn't happen during a game. In drills at practice, T.J. would even swipe his hand at our quarterback when Big Ben dropped back to throw, damn near hitting him. T.J. didn't make contact, but he came close; he was practicing the rep of going after the ball. Ben got it. The pressure from T.J. also allowed *him* to work on avoiding the rush.

I was never that good at punching the ball free. Instead, I used my speed to run by the runner and grab his arm, taking the ball from him. They say that, in the boxing ring, the punch that knocks a fighter out is the one he never sees coming. In football, turnovers happen when the ball carrier stops thinking about keeping possession of the rock because he's distracted by getting tackled or by fighting for another yard or two. That was when I'd strike.

The guys who force turnovers are the guys, like me and T.J., who practice it every single day. We trained our turnover muscle memory to the point that it was second nature. Every second we were on the field, we were conditioned to do all we could to get the ball back for our offense.

As my second season wore on, I continued coming into my own. In a late-season win over Denver, I had six tackles, three pass deflections, and an interception. Against Baltimore, I had thirteen tackles, six of them solo. I went for three solo tackles, three deflections, and my first career interception in a 34–27 win over Denver.

By season's end, I'd played in twelve regular-season games—up four from my rookie year. I had eighty-seven tackles, 3.5 sacks, and that interception. When we played the Bengals in the AFC wild card game in January 2016, I had nine tackles and two forced fumbles, which included stripping the ball from Jeremy Hill with one minute thirty-six seconds left, leading to the game-winning field goal. Talk about making your own luck: just before that play, I'd screamed on the sideline to my defensive teammates, *"Let's go get this ball back!"*

Next up came Denver in the divisional-round play-off. Peyton Manning might have been, at thirty-nine, a shadow of the passer he once was—but he was still a great field general. The game was a hard-hitting defensive battle until the fourth quarter, when my old college teammate Bradley Roby forced a fumble from our backup running back Fitzgerald Toussaint. Manning seized the opportunity and led the Broncos to their only touchdown of the day with three minutes left, sealing a heartbreaking 23–16 loss.

Afterward, the locker room was cold and silent. Every once in a while you could hear a muttered curse or a stifled sob. And then Coach Tomlin was right there among us, tears streaming down his face. Man, sitting there, seeing my head coach feeling the pain with all of us, all I wanted was to burst back out onto that field and do something to wipe those tears away.

* * *

You could make the case that I played for two of the greatest coaches of all time: Urban Meyer and Mike Tomlin. At first glance, they might seem to be as different as could be. Where Coach Meyer was intense and straitlaced, Coach Tomlin was laid-back and warm.

But they were more alike than they seemed. Both were brilliant football tacticians, great x's-and-o's strategists. And they shared a mind-blowing level of attention to detail. Many coaches see themselves as a chief executive, a type of delegator in chief. But Meyer and Tomlin both had their hands in all aspects of their respective teams.

Coach Tomlin would meet with the linebackers and defensive backs about three times a week, just to make sure we were all on the same page. On Fridays, he'd hold what he called our "winning edge" meeting, in which he'd go over every little thing we'd learned about our opponent all week. That's three forty-five-minute meetings with your head coach from which we emerged with no questions about the upcoming game plan.

And while building a game plan is important, both Meyer and Tomlin knew that coaching is also about finding a way to get the absolute most out of your players. Both were master motivators.

Coach Meyer was exactly the coach I needed as a college player. Tough, no-nonsense, stoic. He'd lay down the rules and make it clear that everybody had to follow them; no one was irreplaceable. With all his mind games, he was the patriarch I was desperate to please. He knew which buttons to push for each player. Every day was a test—and you'd find out about your own resilience based on how you reacted to Coach Meyer's tight-lipped remarks.

Coach Tomlin, on the other hand, was more like a father figure. He knew everybody's strengths and weaknesses and he'd adjust how he dealt with you based on what he thought you needed from him to get better. He treated every player like a man, with dignity and respect. He coached with a scalpel rather than a cleaver.

And Coach Tomlin, like his general manager, was emotionally intelligent. So many NFL players, especially those who are African American, are either fatherless or estranged from their fathers, and Coach Tomlin had long filled that role for a lot of guys. Even though he was still only in his forties—he won the 2008 Super Bowl at the age of thirty-six—he kind of reminded me of the old head in the neighborhood that all the young bloods look up to and respect.

All those times I'd get to the practice facility by 6 a.m. to watch film? Often it would be just me and Coach Tomlin in the building, and we'd sit there talking. Family, God, football. He'd hear about R.J.'s restlessness as bedtime approached, and I'd hear about his son's college aspirations. As we grew closer, I even started attending his son's high school football and basketball games.

Soon, every morning he was spending about thirty or forty minutes walking me through what that week's opposing team's offense would be trying to do and what he needed our defense to do in response. We'd go position by position on defense, and I'd learn everybody's assignment. That's how Dad brought me up to play the game; even in high school, I knew where all of my teammates were supposed to be on every defensive play in every game. Coach's son, right?

Football is a game of chess between two coaches, and the extension of each coach on the field is his quarterback. That's why Coach Tomlin and Ben were so tight. But not every coach has a *defensive* quarterback out there, someone who knows at all times what the coach wants and can make calls on the fly to get it done. So once I started calling the defensive plays in my third season, if we were in a Cover 3 defense and the quarterback barked out an audible, I'd know from our early-morning meetings to counter with a blitz. Or if the audible indicated to me that the quarterback had picked up our blitz from the left side, I'd call out a signal to switch it to the opposite side.

Coach Tomlin trusted me; Coach Meyer trusted no one. In some ways, they were both right for where they were. Coach Meyer was a great college coach, which required more of an authoritarian approach. And Coach Tomlin was a great pro coach, who, by treating his players like men, made them want to bust their butts for him.

When Coach Tomlin talked, folks listened. The dude could give a locker room speech that had us practically bursting through the walls. He pulled

141

quotes from popular movies and poems to get us fired up, and he had a reservoir of catchphrases that all drove home the mission of team, sayings like: "More grounded, more humble, more selfless makes us more opportunistic." Or this one: "Iron sharpens iron." Or this: "The time's coming when we're going to have to ante up and kick in like men," he'd say, quoting from the 1989 film *Glory*, about a Black Civil War infantry battalion, which he'd seen twenty-five times.

That last one was no surprise, because Coach Tomlin was always talking about books and movies about wartime. His favorite was *Flags of Our Fathers*, a book written by the son of a US soldier at Iwo Jima. He made it a point not to conflate football with military battle, mind you, but he stressed that the emphases on team camaraderie, on strategy, and on being willing to die for your brother were common to both. The more he talked about these things, the more he infused a locker room with a sense of common purpose and shared adventure, a culture that made for winning football, as evidenced by one stunning statistic: to date, in his fourteen-year NFL coaching career, Mike Tomlin has not had one season with a losing record. Not one.

Coach Tomlin grew up in Newport News, Virginia, the same area that once produced Allen Iverson. His mother and grandfather both worked at, and retired from, the shipyards there. In his office, there's an aerial photo on the wall of his hometown's city streets.

"I used to pick my mom up from work," Tomlin once recalled. "I'd watch everybody spill out of those gates, trying to get on those buses and get out of there. It's a very blue-collar town. But being from there, you have a great amount of pride in it. We are hardened when we come from there."

Is it any wonder, then, that Coach Tomlin succeeded in Pittsburgh, with *its* deep blue-collar roots? Some of his sayings spoke to that hard work ethic that can be found in the salt-of-the-earth folks who have to shower *after* work. "It's a fine line between drinking wine and squashing grapes," he'd say. And while some fans and pundits have criticized him for being "soft" on players, he led with a no-BS practicality that most people who work for a living appreciate: "I'll tolerate you until I can replace you," he liked to say.

After two seasons in the league, I got that Coach Tomlin wasn't thinking of replacing me. He and Coach Butler—now our defensive coordinator—both let it be known that the only thing stopping me from being a Pro Bowl player was that, so far, I'd only played in 62 percent of my team's regular-season games. They showed their faith in me by making me the defensive play-caller. And that made me want to get after it even more.

That's when, while tooling around in my Porsche Panamera, Jerome, Michelle, Vernon II, and I came up with our slogan to turn the whole Burgh into a city of *Shalievers*. And it's when, at James Harrison's suggestion, I hightailed it with Jerome to Scottsdale, where Ian Danney trained both of us at his five-star facility in his unique, holistic training program.

First, I underwent a detailed battery of tests designed to unearth just how my body was compensating for previous injuries, messing with my mechanics. And then we targeted my physical weaknesses and imbalances while strengthening what was already strong. Proper nutrition and supplements were added to my diet.

Jerome prepared for our return to the Burgh by always taking notes. When we got back, it would be time to finish the work of rebuilding my body, mind, and spirit. It was go time.

* * *

Our 2016 season opened before the nation on *Monday Night Football*. At first, it wasn't an auspicious debut. We were trailing 6–0 when Big Ben was sacked and stripped of the ball by Washington linebacker Ryan Kerrigan, who seemed to recover it. But our center, Maurkice Pouncey, knocked the ball out of Kerrigan's hands, and Ben dove on it at our own thirteen-yard line.

Every football game has its moments like these—moments when, looking back on it, you can see the momentum shift. Washington was about to go up two scores on us when we were lucky enough to fall on that ball. As so often happens when crisis is averted, we rallied.

Ben led us on an eighty-seven-yard drive, finishing with a twenty-nine-yard touchdown pass to Antonio Brown on a gutsy fourth-and-one call from the Washington twenty-nine. The next time he got the ball, Ben marched us downfield sixty-seven yards. Suddenly we were ahead, 14–6.

For my part, it felt like I made a statement with six tackles, two pass deflections, a forced fumble, and an interception of Washington quarterback Kirk Cousins in the 38–16 rout. In the third quarter, back-to-back plays told the story of the linebacker I'd become. On the first, I made a tackle and forced a fumble, which Washington recovered. No problem—I just had to figure out *another* way to deliver for my teammates. The next play, I read Cousins's eyes from the pocket and picked him off. That set up another Ben-to-Antonio scoring hookup. Game over.

Next up was Cincinnati. It had barely been eight months since I'd forced two fumbles against them in last season's wild card game. Now, in week two, here were the Bengals again, a division rival. I had twelve tackles in a 24–16 win.

I'd always known I could play, but there's a difference between that kind of confidence and the swagger I was bringing to every play now. Every time I strapped on a helmet, there was a hop to my step, because I knew I was the most prepared man on the field.

I'd become obsessed with getting better. I'd seen guys have a great stretch of games only to let up on the accelerator. I was damn sure that wasn't going to happen to me. Remember *kaizen*, the Japanese culture of continual improvement? Sure, things were going great *now* on the field, but if you're not moving forward, you're going to get left behind. What else could I do?

In our early-morning coffees together, I'd quiz Coach Tomlin, looking for any edge I could find. I'd go to Roethlisberger and pick his brain about what we as a defense were up against. I'd ask him about opposing quarterbacks: What made Brady so good? How should we think about containing Rodgers?

I remember Ben walking me through what I should be thinking about when trying to read the quarterback. As a linebacker, I focused on the stripe down the center of the quarterback's helmet, because it told me where he was looking. If the stripe was facing left, he couldn't throw to the right—so now I only had to defend half the field. Well, Ben explained, a young quarterback might try to look you off to the right once before coming back to his receiver on the left, but a veteran like Cincinnati's Andy Dalton knows he actually has more time than that; he'll look to his right on his drop back, then turn his head to the left to get the defense to shift that way, and then—once he sees you've bitten—he'll come back to a receiver on the right side. Younger quarterbacks will look right at where they're throwing to; veterans will look in two or three different directions before throwing, just to keep you off base.

I'd also ask our offensive coaches to break down *my* game. If you were facing me, what would you tell your offense about how to attack me? One coach explained to me that, if I'm lined up against a 250-pound tight end on an up-and-out route, I do what most linebackers do: I backpedal, we have contact, and then the tight end cuts and runs toward the sideline. "If you're a linebacker and someone who is 250 pounds hits you, you're gonna move," one of the offensive coaches told me, "so you're helping him create space." I learned instead to stay just behind the receiver, eyeing his hip so I knew when the cut was about to come, and then use my speed to recover and "jump the route"—cut in between the receiver and the ball—at the last possible instant.

Meantime, my old nemesis—injury—made another visit. In week one, I'd sprained the MCL in my knee. No big deal. But in our third game, Philadelphia and its rookie quarterback, Carson Wentz, shellacked us, and my sprain was aggravated. I was all about willing myself to greatness, but there are some things that just don't care about the power of your will. I had to sit out three games while undergoing treatment and helping my knee to heal.

Around the same time that I went out, Ben tore the meniscus in *his* knee and was sidelined until week nine. We had jumped out of the gate with a 4–1 record, but soon we began a four-game losing streak. We were 4–5 in a season that had begun with such high hopes. Fans and media were calling for Coach Tomlin's job. Pittsburgh might have loved the guy, but a football fan's love is easily tested when the going gets rough.

But here's why you should never doubt a Mike Tomlin team: because, as the Stoics would tell you, the obstacle is the way. Coach Tomlin got up in our grill: Were we going to rise to this challenge? He stoked an us-versus-them mentality. Outsiders had given up on us, he said. "But the guys inside this locker room? *They never give up. Now let's go prove the doubters wrong.*" Suddenly we were full of hope and belief—and, well, anger. Resentment can be a great motivator.

It helped that Ben and I were back at full strength. We finished the regular season by reeling off seven wins in a row. We clinched the division title on Christmas Day at home against the Ravens. I had ten tackles and picked off Joe Flacco in a 31–27 win.

In fact, all that turnover muscle memory work was paying off. The next three games, I picked off passes. Next came a pick against Robert Griffin III in our regular-season finale. In the AFC wild card game, we routed the Dolphins; I intercepted Matt Moore and we held Miami's star runner, Jay Ajayi, to thirty-three yards on sixteen carries.

The AFC divisional playoff game would be the kind of throwback I loved: good, hard-hitting, defensive football. It was cold and rainy at Arrowhead Stadium—

classic old-school football weather. The Chiefs were coached by Andy Reid, who I'd place right up there with Coach Tomlin as one of the best in the game.

This would be a grind-out game, and Le'Veon Bell would shred the KC defense for 170 rushing yards, despite playing through a groin injury. KC's defense bent but wouldn't break. They held us to six field goals by kicker Chris Boswell, the most made in an NFL playoff game. We won the turnover battle, 2–1; I picked off Chiefs quarterback Alex Smith after my linebacker mate Bud Dupree hit his arm while throwing—another big play. We were the first team in NFL history to win a divisional round playoff game without scoring a touchdown. That's the definition of gutsy.

That set up a showdown with New England for the right to go to the Super Bowl. We'd had many face-offs against the Patriots through the years, but this felt different. We were on a roll, and we'd have our full complement of "Killer Bs" on the field: Ben, Bell, and (Antonio) Brown.

But not for long. Le'Veon came into the game on a roll, having gone for 167 yards against Miami before running wild against the Chiefs. But he took a painkilling shot for that groin injury before the Patriots game. He felt great in warm-ups, but the first time he took a hit, the pain returned, worse than ever. Late in the first quarter, he left the game for good. And we were cooked.

Tom Brady picked us apart. When we blitzed, he

picked it up. And when we didn't, he was content to sit in the pocket and dissect us. We lost for the first time in ten weeks, 36–17. Le'Veon would later tell *Sports Illustrated*, "2016 was our Super Bowl year. I just got hurt."

I had eighty-seven regular-season tackles for the second consecutive year, along with 3.5 sacks, three interceptions, and three forced fumbles. As good as those statistics might seem, I don't think the game has ever really come up with a smart way to statistically judge defensive players. I was actually most proud of a statistic few knew: apparently, I was one of the best in the league in getting ball carriers down on the ground quickly.

According to the website Pro Football Focus, I allowed the fewest yards (1.08) in the NFL in 2016 after making first contact against runs. Behind me were two defensive linemen—Aaron Donald of the Los Angeles Rams and Malik Jackson of the Jacksonville Jaguars. Forty-three of my tackles came against the run, and eighteen of those were unassisted. In addition, I led the Steelers in total run tackles for a loss, with eight.

To me, those statistics showed just how much I contributed to our team effort. It's one thing to be part of a group tackle. It's another to consistently bring down an opposing runner by yourself, time and again.

While it might not have been widely known how often I'd done just that, smart football observers sensed what I was doing. That's why I was named to the Pro Bowl for the first time. Still, each season only has one winner: the eventual Super Bowl champion. I couldn't wait till next year.

* * *

In the off-season, Dad and I had our annual talk on his front porch in Fort Lauderdale, which is where he does all his best thinking, usually with a cigar dangling from his lips. The conversation was the same one we'd been having since I first suited up for pee wee football. I'd share with him my goals—and outline exactly what I was willing to sacrifice in order to achieve them.

I think my goal for 2017 surprised even Dad. It wasn't just to return to the Pro Bowl. Or to win the Super Bowl. Or to stay healthy. Yeah, my goals included all those things, but I had a bigger vision.

I knew it was crazy, but I'd always set crazy goals. I wanted to be like Ray Lewis and play in the league for seventeen years. I wanted to establish a new standard for the modern-day linebacker. I wanted to be a first-ballot Hall of Famer.

Lofty goals? Yes. But what's the sense of dreaming if you don't dream big? After all, my track record on making dreams come true was pretty good. And I just knew that 2017 was shaping up to be a defining season for me.

As training camp opened, there was more excitement

for a season than I could recall—and that's saying something for Pittsburgh. Our offense was lethal, behind Ben, Le'Veon Bell, Antonio Brown, and wide receiver Martavis Bryant, who had been suspended through all of the previous season for violating the league's substance abuse policy.

On defense, I led a healthy returning roster of veterans that included Cam Heyward, Bud Dupree, Sean Davis, and Artie Burns. There was also my man Vince Williams, my fellow linebacker. I was tighter with Vince than anyone else on the team.

It hadn't always been like that. When the Steelers first drafted me in the first round in the 2014 draft, Vince saw me as a threat. He'd been drafted the year before, in the sixth round. It didn't sit well with him that I was named a starter over him right away.

But in the off-season after my rookie year, a bunch of us rented a house together to work out in. The other guys would fly home on weekends, and Vince and I would work out like crazy together—intense two-a-days—and then hang out afterward. We'd compete against one another, and soon a mutual respect took hold.

We were very different. Vince was laid-back; I was more of a socializer. But our love for the game was a bond. Soon it was like we each knew what the other was thinking on the field at all times.

Now, we both had high hopes for the 2017 season. So much so, I told him we needed to adopt a nickname together. I could see it blowing up, going viral. Vince was skeptical. Every name I threw out—"Splash and Dash," "Thunder and Lightning"—he rejected.

One day, we hit on it. Vince and I spent a lot of our free time together watching movies. We'd go to movie theaters, but we'd also watch them on a big screen at my house. Once, flipping through channels, we came across *Talladega Nights*, starring Will Ferrell as NASCAR racing sensation Ricky Bobby and John C. Reilly as his partner, Cal Naughton Jr. Ricky Bobby dubs them "Shake and Bake" because those are "two verbs, they go good together, and they rhyme."

The next day, Vince and I were in the car when I dropped it on him. "I've got our nickname, bro," I said. "'Shake and Bake,' like in *Talladega Nights*!"

Vince was not that enthusiastic at first, but it grew on him. "Man," I said, "if you smell a delicious crispy smell in the stadium, it ain't your corn dog, it's Shake—"

"—and Bake!" Vince said finishing my thought, just like on the field.

It made sense. Vince was a hard hitter who liked to bake people up. I'm more the shifty one, shaking around, speedily making plays. We had a lot of fun doing a video for the Steelers Facebook page to introduce our new nickname. And it caught on—soon, everywhere we went, fans were calling me "Shake" and Vince "Bake."

Meanwhile, the stage was set for a big season. "There are no unknowns for those guys," Coach Tomlin said of our returning defensive lineup at our training camp in Latrobe, Pennsylvania. "They've been in Latrobe before. They know where these roads lead, so it should be reflected in their readiness and in their play."

Sometimes teams just have a championship air about them. We had a veteran group that was going to lead the league in being competitors. That ethic came from Coach Tomlin, but it also came from our captains. On defense, our captain was Cam Heyward, a loud, take-no-prisoners voice in the locker room. I was the defensive signal-caller, but I was a quieter leader than Cam, which was why I'd voted for him to be captain. He had a way of making you want to follow him into a foxhole.

Like me, Ben was a quiet leader, but he might have been the most competitive dude I'd ever played with. He competed at everything, and when your quarterback is that guy, the team starts to take on that same type of tough-mindedness. At practice on Thursdays and Fridays, we had a drill called "7 Shots." The offense would line up at the goal line and go against the defense for seven straight plays—the first to get to four touchdowns or four stops would be the winner.

Man, those were offense-versus-defense wars—as intense as anything we'd do come Sunday. Once, we stopped them four straight times, sealing our win. Then, just to rub it in, we simply stood there for the last three now-meaningless plays. Ben looked like he was ready to wipe our smiles off our faces by throwing down with all of us, and the coaches weren't that pleased with our taunting behavior, either.

But that supercharged competitive atmosphere was our secret sauce as the 2017 season got underway. We carried ourselves with a not-so-quiet confidence. In week one, I had eleven solo tackles and forced two fumbles in a 21–18 win over Cleveland. It felt like a prophecy.

We hadn't won in Baltimore since 2012, but in week four we waltzed into Raven country and made a statement with a 26–9 win. In the fourth quarter, we were leading 19–9 when I picked off Baltimore quarterback Joe Flacco. When the Ravens got the ball back, they went for it on fourth down. I blitzed and got my hand on Flacco's pass, tipping it in the air. Cornerback Mike Hilton came down with it, sealing the win.

In week ten versus Indianapolis, we struggled. Early in the fourth quarter, down 17–9 to a 3–6 team, I was trying to rally my teammates in the huddle to come up with a big play. We needed to give Ben and the guys a chance to get us back in this thing.

On third and eight from his own thirteen, Colts quarterback Jacoby Brissett threw a quick out to tight end Jack Doyle. The ball bounced off Doyle's hands while I was lining him up for a big hit. I had to adjust in midair, and I corralled my hands around the ball before it fell to the ground. I'd given possession of the ball back to my offense; after they punched it in and made the two-point conversion, we were all tied up, setting the stage for a last-second game-winning field goal by Chris Boswell.

The next week, we faced a team that would eventually reach the second round of the playoffs, the Tennessee Titans. I had ten tackles, we intercepted quarterback Marcus Mariota four times, and we held the Titan offense to fifty-two yards on twenty-one attempts in a 40–17 romp.

With an 8–2 record, we were on a roll. Before our next game, against Green Bay, even Coach Tomlin couldn't contain himself. In an interview, he stated outright that he thought we were good enough to win the Super Bowl. And he said he was looking forward to New England's visit to Heinz Field on December 17—the one that would end in that terrible call ruling Jesse James's catch incomplete when it had seemed to be the game-winning touchdown.

Coach Tomlin's comments looking ahead to that game raised eyebrows, because Coach Tomlin was never about looking past your next opponent. But there's always a method to his madness. I think at the time he wanted us to know he believed in us, *and* he wanted to challenge us to live up to his expectations. The previous year, we hadn't talked about our hopes for the future. We'd followed the familiar "one game at a time" NFL script. How had that worked out for us?

Now, Coach Tomlin acknowledged the elephant in the room. When pressed on his comments about the New England game as a Super Bowl litmus test, he just told it like it was. "We've got a good football team," Tomlin said. "I've got a great deal of confidence in them. Everybody in America knows it's a big game. We couldn't deny it if we wanted to."

First, though, we had a date with the Green Bay Packers. Aaron Rodgers was injured, but backup quarterback Brett Hundley led an inspired upset effort. I had eight tackles, and a whole lot of near misses when it came to getting to Hundley. The game was tied at 28 with seventeen seconds left when Ben and his boys took over. Antonio Brown made a miraculous twenty-three-yard catch on the sideline, which set up our clutch kicker, Chris Boswell, who nailed a fifty-three-yarder for the win at the buzzer.

We were 9–2. I had mildly sprained my ankle chasing Hundley, but it didn't seem like anything that would keep me from suiting up the next week, at Cincinnati on *Monday Night Football*. It was tempting to think beyond the Bengals, especially with the Patriots looming in the not-so-distant future.

Michelle saw how swollen my ankle had gotten. "Maybe you shouldn't play," she said, noting that we'd already clinched the division. "Maybe you should rest."

"Nah, it's fine. I gotta be there for my teammates."

We were on a mission: Super Bowl or bust. *Cincinnati, here we come.*

CHAPTER NINE
THE COMEBACK

It had been a little over six months since I lay on the turf of Cincinnati's Paul Brown Stadium amid that hushed silence. And I still hadn't publicly spoken. Oh, I'd had public *moments*: There were appearances at a couple of Steelers games, and the twenty-eight-step walk at the NFL Draft to announce the Steelers pick. There was the Penguins hockey game where the arena erupted in a standing ovation when my face appeared on the fan-o-vision and I stood up on my own.

But I still hadn't *talked* publicly about all that I'd been through. That changed in June 2018, when I decided to hold a press conference at the Steelers facility.

Interview requests from the media had been piling up. Why hadn't I spoken? In part, I think I didn't know what to say. I was still finding my way in this new reality. But I also instinctively wanted to control my own story. Remember how I didn't want to get married when I thought I might look unhappy in the wedding pictures? Well, I also didn't want to look back at video of a press conference and see a depressed athlete talking about his injury. If I was going to speak publicly, I wanted to be sure that I was projecting positivity.

And there was one other thing driving me to want to speak: man, I was overflowing with gratitude. Just saying thank you every day to everyone who was doing so much for me—my family, the docs, the folks at UPMC and Mercy, my teammates, Jerome—wasn't enough. I felt the need to publicly express how grateful I felt to the fans and city of Pittsburgh itself, and how humbled.

Again, the Stoics had something to do with this urge. "He is a wise man who does not grieve for the things which he has not, but rejoices for those which he has," wrote Epictetus.

By now I was walking, very gingerly, with a cane. And my days were full: I'd be at the practice facility to work out by 6 a.m. and then watch film with the scouts and coaches; I'd jot down notes, taking in just how they broke down tape and devised plays. Then I'd sit in on defensive team meetings and do PT treatment in the afternoon. At night, Jerome would come over after dinner, and we'd do a strenuous two-hour workout together to close out the day. I'd try to get to sleep by 10 p.m., though sometimes *Fortnite* had something to say about that.

That jam-packed routine was something to be thankful for, as was each tentative step I took each day. In fact, I was learning that it's pretty much impossible to be grateful and depressed or sad or angry at the same time. Turns out, that conclusion has been backed up by science. In *Thanks!: How the New Science of Gratitude Can Make You Happier*, psychologist Robert Emmons cites study after study showing that people who stop and take the time to recognize the things they're thankful for experience more positive emotions, feel more alive, sleep better, express more compassion and kindness, and even have stronger immune systems.

I felt like I was bursting with gratefulness, and I was coming to believe that the expression of it was as much a part of my recovery as every left leg extension rep in the gym.

A lot of familiar faces filled the Steelers' postgame press room. Wearing a neatly pressed black button-down shirt, I stood at a podium in front of a backdrop with the Steelers and PNC Bank logos on it. Funny, all those times I'd played football before hundreds of thousands of people—millions if you count everyone watching on TV—and I'm not sure I'd ever been *that* nervous before. I'd prepared a few remarks, but mostly I was just going to wing it and speak from the heart.

I started by thanking all those around me, including Michelle, my parents, and R.J. The doctors and staff at UPMC and Mercy. The Steelers—Mr. Rooney, Coach

Tomlin, Kevin Colbert, my teammates. The list went on. I thanked those in Cincinnati—"I know, when this happened, it was scary to people there, too, at first"—and then I addressed Steeler Nation directly: "The prayers that you have been praying out for me, I can really feel it when I'm going through rehab, I can really feel it throughout the day, and it's just pushing me to continue to go harder and get better every single day."

My gratitude list was long, and I didn't want to leave anybody out. "When I was in Mercy, I was getting so many letters," I said, "and I'm just so thankful....I had an elementary school, every single kid in the whole school wrote me a get well soon letter. That's over five hundred kids. All that feeds to make me want to do better."

I opened the floor to questions. The first one was predictable: Did I plan on playing again? "Yeah, my dream is to come back and play football again. I have been working my tail off every single day. I have that in the back of my mind every single time I go to rehab. You know, I just try to stay positive and do everything I can to get back."

A reporter wanted to know if I was ever scared. "I'm not going to lie, I was a little scared when it happened, but I just trusted the Lord and asked him to watch over my life," I said. "I know He has a bigger purpose."

When someone asked if I was different now, I

nodded. "You definitely appreciate everything a lot more now—taking my first step, walking at the draft, even just standing here now and talking to you....Honestly, I appreciate every moment I'm in. When I was in rehab, the first few steps I took, I'm not going to lie, me and my family were crying. When I look back at my videos, I still cry, but it's all tears of joy."

I had recently read that Magic Johnson, when he was first diagnosed with the virus that causes AIDS, was told by his doctors that his attitude was going to be an important factor in his recovery. "If you're telling me that I can beat this thing with a positive attitude," he said, "then it's over. I've got it beaten."

At the time the virus was seen to be a death sentence, but today, roughly thirty years later, Magic Johnson is a symbol of resilience and good health. I wanted to make sure everyone understood the power of positive thinking. "Ever since I was young, I believed that if you have a positive mindset, you'll have a good outcome," I said. "Now I just try and have that positive mindset because a lot of times you take things for granted that you don't think you take for granted."

Now that I stood there in front of the press, the butterflies were gone. I felt like a burden had been lifted. I'd been dying to tell the world about all the folks—like the kids at that elementary school—who had made such a difference in my life. All those people who prayed for me, people I'd never even met? What they did *mattered*. Every time I looked at my *"Walking Miracle"* bracelet, courtesy of my godmother, Robina, it reinforced my belief that God had heard and answered their prayers.

Remember Adam Taliaferro, the Penn State defensive back who was paralyzed in 1999 and came back to walk again? His coach, the legendary Joe Paterno, whose own son made a full recovery from a near-fatal trampoline accident, made a compelling case for the power of prayer in the book that chronicled Adam's comeback. "I know a lot of people don't believe there's such a thing as miracles anymore," Paterno said. "But it's hard to believe there isn't some kind of force up there, that when so many people are concerned about somebody that it doesn't have an impact. To me, I keep thinking I've been involved with some people that I care for who have literally had someone step in and create a miracle."

My gratitude wasn't just for all those individuals I didn't know who had prayed for me. It was also for the city of Pittsburgh itself. A lot of athletes don't become citizens of the cities where they play; they come from somewhere else to do their job and move back home after their playing days. They're rent-a-jocks. And that's cool—no one says you have to be more engaged than that. But I'd always wanted to be a part of the Pittsburgh community, where the Rooney family has a long-standing reputation for acts of faith and giving back.

That's why, when I was invited to be honored at the Art Rooney Award Dinner, I jumped at the chance. Since the 1970s, the dinner has benefited the Catholic Youth Organization and honors Pittsburgh's "champions"—those who have made a difference in the community and display a passion for Pittsburgh. The dinner pays tribute to the legacy of Art Rooney Sr. and is still run by his grandson, Steelers president Art Rooney II.

For me, the dinner was an opportunity to once again pay homage to my adopted hometown. "I consider myself a Yinzer," I said. "It means a lot because I know the whole city has my back in every form, when it comes to sports, life, on a daily basis. I am thankful Mr. Rooney thinks I represent the city and the sports here."

I'd been raised to be polite, so I'd always said thank you to folks. But now those words were feeling hollow. All the nurses who bathed me, all the physical therapists who tried every which way to get my lower extremities to wake up? A mere thank-you to them would never be enough. But I could take advantage of my platform and call wide attention to all the unknown heroes like them who are among us every day.

That's especially true of the caregivers. Sometimes I think they're the ones who are too often easily forgotten. Mom, Dad, and Michelle went above and beyond, yes, but trust me: they were doing what family members in every room of every hospital are doing every day across the nation. Throughout the country, sixty-five million people provide care for an injured or disabled loved one, and half of them battle depression. Their stress is overwhelming. In 2009, the AARP valued the unpaid labor of family caregivers at $450 billion per year. Those who take on caring for spinal cord injury patients are seldom talked about, but they're the true angels in this fight.

That day, driving back home with *my* angel, I held Michelle's hand and told her I felt lighter now that the fans had finally seen and heard from me.

* * *

An NFL locker room is a kind of sacred space. It's the meeting place for so many different types of people, all united around a common goal. I've dressed alongside preacher's sons, Muslims, good ole boys from down South, and rebels without a cause. It's a trip, because what you learn is that it really *does* take all kinds. Winning is all about accepting the difference in your brother, loving him anyway, holding hands in the huddle, and then kicking ass together on Sunday.

Teams in the NFL have all sorts of folks who come into the locker room—docs, executives, equipment managers. But they're not *of* the locker room. The guys you go to war with on Sunday—*that's* who makes up the locker room. With those guys, I sobbed after tough losses. With them, I got into face-to-face screaming matches, demanding accountability on the field—followed by the brotherly act of hugging it out.

But when injured, most players feel like they've been banished from that culture. Oh, they still have locker room privileges, but if you ain't suiting up, you're suddenly an outsider. You're the mess tent sergeant—you still have a supportive role, but you're not part of the intimate closeness that comes from being on the front lines. And if you're not in the foxhole, you can start to feel like a fan with really good access.

Well, after my injury in Cincinnati, I *never* felt that way. My teammates wouldn't let me. This is what's so special about Pittsburgh and a Mike Tomlin team. As the 2018 season got underway, I was at every practice, in every team meeting, and I was a vocal part of every conversation about our mission. I was not only on the sidelines for every game but in every sideline defensive huddle. It wasn't some feel-good accommodation by my teammates, either. They wanted me with them. If I couldn't lead them on the actual field, I could be part of leading them in every other way imaginable.

A lot of times, active players don't want severely injured players around them. They're a flesh-and-blood reminder of the risks players face every day on the field. But not my teammates. In fact, a number of them thanked me for what *I* was doing for *them* by being around. I was showing up and working out with a smile on my face every day. I was modeling resilience.

In fact, I was still keeping my playing schedule. Jerome and I would get to the facility by 6 a.m. to work out, and afterward I'd watch film, often with Coach Tomlin and the assistant coaches. I'd chime in on game-plan decisions and attend our defensive team meetings. I'd be there at practice, offering tips and suggestions. Come game time, I'd be on the sideline, huddling with the defense when Ben and his boys had the ball.

I had a foot in both worlds. I was kind of like an assistant coach, though I was still one of the guys. If a teammate had an issue, he could come to me and I'd figure out a way to bring it up the chain without ruffling anyone's feathers.

And the 2018 season had its share of issues. It was a wild season. We were 1–2–1 after four games, but then we reeled off six wins in a row. Then we fell apart, losing four of our last six to finish at 9–6–1 and miss the playoffs for the first time since the year before my rookie season.

There were a lot of reasons for the collapse, but much of it had to do with internal team chemistry. On paper, the Steelers were stacked. Ben finished the season with the most passing yards in the NFL, 5,129, and thirty-four touchdowns, sixteen interceptions, and a 96.5 passer rating. Antonio Brown ended with 1,297 yards and fifteen touchdowns, while fellow star wide receiver JuJu Smith-Schuster put up 1,426 yards and seven touchdowns.

But Le'Veon Bell ended up holding out for the whole year in hopes of landing a better contract. And the relationship between Ben and Antonio Brown blew up late in the season: Antonio, upset by something Ben had said or done, walked out of a practice and, as a result, was benched for the final regular-season game. After the season, Antonio tweeted about his quarterback: "He has an owner mentality like he can call out anybody including coaches. Players know but they can't say anything about it otherwise they meal ticket gone. It's a dirty game within a game."

What hurt me the most, though, was how our defense contributed to our underachievement. There were bright spots—like my man T.J. Watt, who had thirteen sacks in his second season—but we gave up 22.5 points per game, seventeenth in the NFL. And, in those last six games, we surrendered nearly four hundred yards per game.

It killed me to see our defense pushed around like that, and it made me feel helpless. But it also made my comeback much more urgent. My teammates needed me.

* * *

Fight through it, Ryan. You got this. Fight through it.

In the past, that's what I'd say to myself during two-a-day workouts in the hot sun, when I couldn't see because of the buckets of sweat cascading down my face off my forehead, when every breath felt like it was the last I had to give. Now, I was saying it while *walking* on a treadmill.

That's the funny part: it actually took more fight and will and stamina to walk on a treadmill in the six months after my injury than it ever did to leave it all on the practice field as an NFL player. That's because, on the treadmill, I was fighting my own body. My muscles, which had gradually awakened in the first three months after the injury, now had a short shelf life. I'd have to push them to exhaustion and then beyond. I had to work them into shape before even thinking about the process of recovering their lost memory.

In other words, before seeing if I was capable of football movements, I'd have to get my body strong enough to even try them. By the start of the 2018 season, I was walking without the cane, tentatively at first. I still had that significant hitch in my gait coming from my left hip. It just hadn't caught up yet to my right side.

There were still places below my navel where I didn't have feeling or had just the faintest, dull sensation when touched.

But I could sense my body making progress every day. Jerome would bark in my ears, always smiling, urging me on. He was my MVP, man, because if I'd been alone I probably would have packed up shop much sooner every day than I did. He knew what a competitor I am, so he'd challenge me: "You can do five more minutes on a damn treadmill!" or "C'mon, five more reps and you're done!"

And when Jerome wasn't riding me, Coach Tomlin or Kevin Colbert were stopping by, urging me on. "You only doing ten reps?" Coach might ask. "C'mon. You can do fifteen." I loved it. Every day I'd set mini goals for myself. Fifteen reps when I'd been doing ten—move the chains, 'cause that's a first down.

As the weeks rolled by, I started posting videos of my workouts on Instagram. Invariably, they'd go viral. Obviously, there was still interest in how I was coming along, but I think something deeper was going on, too. Fans don't normally see the work that goes into an athlete's performance on the field. They think we're born with this freakish talent.

Well, the best athletes I know all agree that we couldn't play a lick the first time we tried to. Oh, we may have certain talents—I was always fast; I bet Michael Jordan could always jump high. But remember, even that dude got cut from his high school basketball team. The fact is, we're much more craftsmen than artists. What you see on the field is a product of those ten thousand (or more) hours of practice that author Malcolm Gladwell says raise your chances of achieving expertise.

I think people wanted to see how my comeback was going, yes, but I also think they were drawn to a glimpse behind the curtain. So few fans had ever stopped to realize that what they saw on an NFL Sunday was, rather than the stuff of divine intervention, the product of good old-fashioned hard work. That made them curious about just what went into it—and maybe made them wonder whether *they* could make the same type of commitment.

I wasn't just working out my body. I was also trying to recover from the mental trauma of my injury. That's why, when we played at Cincinnati early in the 2018 season, walking onto the field at Paul Brown Stadium on my own meant the world to me. I walked right to the spot where I'd been injured, where I'd been carried from the field. And I walked away from that spot under my own power. The moment spoke to my teammates, too.

"This is a place that we'll always remember," Ben said after our 28–21 victory, his eyes misting over. "This meant something to us, not just for football, but for life."

Before our game that day, I got the chance to walk on my own through the doors of the University of Cincinnati Medical Center, where I'd been taken only ten months before. I was met by so many loving faces. I didn't remember every single person, but so many crowded around me, and some even thanked *me* for coming back to thank *them*.

Remember gratitude? Man, being able to say thank you to those docs and nurses made *me* feel great. And I meant it, because in spinal cord injury cases, often the difference between walking again or spending your life in a wheelchair is determined by how the patient is treated in the very first hours. If the inflammation can be controlled and lessened shortly after injury, the odds of recovery are much higher. Dr. O had told them to try everything, and the folks at UC Medical Center ended up doing everything right—and they did it quickly.

Before the season ended, I posted a video of myself cleanly deadlifting 150 pounds, with the caption, *"Through the pain and the success. You must always remain* HUMBLE.*"*

I'd been thinking a lot about humility. I thought I'd always been humble; I'd certainly been brought up that way. But, cruising around the Burgh in my Porsche Panamera, an NFL All-Pro, had I gotten kind of cocky? I liked thinking about the injury as God's way of telling me that, as His child, He wanted me to be more intentionally grateful.

And if that meant that videos of me working out could inspire others, posting them was the least I could do. A few months after the season ended, I posted a video of myself doing a standing box jump onto a three-foot box. It had not even been nineteen months since my injury. I captioned the video with my new formula for success: DEDICATION = HARD WORK + PATIENCE. *Those* are the values that win in football, and in life.

* * *

Uh-oh. It's never a good sign when your significant other texts you to say you all need to talk. This was back in April 2018; I was working out at the facility when I got the ominous word.

I started wondering what I'd done. I can be a bit messy around the house. Had I left dirty laundry lying around again? Or was something seriously wrong? But I needn't have worried. When I got home, Michelle was sitting at the dining room table, and she was beaming. Michelle has a beautiful smile—it was the first thing that attracted me to her, remember?—but this one was blinding—a *full-body* smile.

"We're pregnant!" she burst out, barely able to contain herself.

I have to admit, I was confused at first, even though she'd already told me that her period was late. But it hadn't been that long ago that we'd had that conversation with Dr. O in which he assured us that my equipment would be working just fine—eventually. But it still wasn't, not consistently. That's one of the things I was learning. Recovery from spinal cord paralysis isn't like flipping a switch. The body recovers in a haphazard way; some days, some muscles respond. Other days, they just don't. I'd experienced it on the treadmill—and in the bedroom.

I could tell this was frustrating Michelle and that she was wondering if our troubles were her fault. Of course they weren't—it was just the situation I was in. But that doubt and insecurity is common in circumstances like ours.

I knew how badly she wanted to get pregnant, and I desperately wanted that, too. But the issue had been kind of hanging over us. We both felt the pressure. I didn't expect we'd be pregnant so soon, especially since I still didn't always have complete sensation below the navel.

Some might scoff at it, but after all we'd been through, you couldn't tell us this wasn't a sign from God. Is there anything more hopeful than news of a pregnancy? Especially at a time when we weren't sure it was even possible. There was no doubt in my mind and soul that this was a divine message. God was saying, *Hey, just continue to believe in Me, continue to follow My path.* Because there had been so many dark days, and now here was God telling me, *Just continue to trust Me and I'll give you all you need.* I don't think I'd ever felt the words of my favorite Bible passage, Psalm 23, more strongly: *Surely goodness and mercy shall follow me all the days of my life: and I will dwell in the house of the Lord forever.*

After jumping into each other's arms, Michelle and I talked about names. I suggested an unconventional choice if our baby was a boy: Lyon. Growing up, I'd always loved lions. They were strong and proud and leaders of their pride. And I liked that the name rhymed with my first name. "I'm not feeling that," Michelle said, looking at me kind of strangely.

But within a day or two, she had a change of heart. "It really does kind of represent everything we've gone through, doesn't it?" she said. "Just constantly believing, striving for greatness."

"Yeah," I said. "For the past year, we've had to fight so hard to get here. That's our lion roar."

She was sold. And our miracle baby, Lyon Carter Shazier, was born in January 2019—just in time to be a very special guest at the wedding of his mother and father.

* * *

Though we'd originally thought we would marry in Miami, now it felt like a no-brainer: we had to hold the event in the Burgh. Obviously we couldn't invite all those who had prayed for us the last eighteen months, but we could at least hold the celebration of our union in the city that had stood by me in the toughest of times.

Michelle was all about planning the wedding. Former Steeler Will Allen was married to a wedding planner named Alexis Allen; Michelle had seen photos of her work on Instagram and felt an instant connection. I reached out to Will for an introduction.

I wasn't very involved after that as Michelle and Alexis hit it off and ran with it. There was an instant bond; Alexis was also a person of deep faith, and she understood how much the wedding meant to so many people. We were celebrating the marriage of two people, sure, but Michelle also wanted to use the occasion to celebrate how far I'd come since my injury. And I thought it was also a good time to honor so many of the folks who had loved us, prayed for us, and stressed out about us over the last year and a half. Weddings are meaningful to begin with, but this one was going to be full of love.

We set the date for May 3, 2019, at the Pennsylvanian in downtown Pittsburgh. It's a Pittsburgh landmark, once part of the city's Penn Station, an eleven-thousand-square-foot event space with arched openings, marble floors, and forty-foot ceilings. I loved that it was iconically Pittsburgh.

I made the arrangements for my tux and kept the details from Michelle. I wanted to drop it on her there. Alexis had introduced me to a local designer named David Alan. I told him I wanted to incorporate a lion logo into the tux, and I wanted to outfit R.J. and Lyon in the same suits. David blew me away with a pink tux with black trim, a lion faintly visible next to the lapel. Man, we were banging—the three Shazier boys.

Michelle wore a light, flowing Oscar de la Renta gown with hand-painted flowers and a matching veil she got from a high-end Miami boutique.

When the day came, Michelle got her first glimpse of the tux when, somehow, R.J. snuck back behind the curtain before she walked down the aisle. "Mimi!" he yelled, running up and hugging her. That's when it hit her—this was really happening! She started crying, dabbing at her eyes to make sure she didn't ruin her makeup.

My father officiated. I could hear the emotion in his voice, but he didn't mention anything about the journey we'd taken to get here. He didn't have to. Everyone knew the story and what this moment meant. I really appreciated that he performed the ceremony as though he were marrying any two of his congregants. After he said I could kiss the bride—and I did—it was time to party.

For the reception, we were introduced for the first time as man and wife to the sound of John Legend's "*A Good Night.*" Very deliberately, there was no seating chart. We were bringing together so many different people from so many different parts of our lives, and Michelle and Alexis wanted people to mingle and meet each other. The guest list included celebrities like Ben Roethlisberger and actor Joe Manganiello, a huge Steelers fan, and his wife, actress Sofia Vergara, so we asked guests to either not bring their cell phones or agree to have them confiscated at the door. Some famous folks might not want their pictures taken and posted to social media when they're kicking back at a friend's wedding.

One of the funniest moments was when my brother, Vernon, rose to offer his best man toast. By then, my man was pretty drunk. To this day, he'll tell you what he said, but no one who was there could make out a word of it. He slurred his way through it. I can't tell you how many of my teammates came up to me and said, "Man, what the hell did Vernon say?"

After Vernon's wild ride of a speech, the party got rocking. Cherry blossom trees surrounded the DJ booth, where Atlanta-based DJ Battle got everyone on the dance floor. There were two cool dinner buffets: Michelle's Puerto Rican Station served chicken-and-pork paella, Cuban sandwiches, and spicy beef, potato, and cheese empanadas; my Southern Comfort Station featured deep-fried chicken and waffles, BBQ pulled pork sandwiches, baked sweet potatoes, green bean casserole, and warm cornbread. But that wasn't all. There was also a catering station with brisket and grits, and an Italian station with ravioli and penne pasta in a cream sauce. Dessert? How about ice cream sandwiches, milkshakes, flan, and guava-glazed cheesecake squares?

As the night wore on, Michelle and I kicked it on the dance floor. Now, I'm not going to say I danced *well*, mind you. I promise, I had a better sense of rhythm before my injury. But who cares—the point was that I could dance at all. (Not long after, a producer from *Dancing with the Stars* asked if I'd take part in the show. Uh, no thanks, bruh). Dr. O later said that he held his breath when I started dancing—that watching me made him more nervous than when he performs surgery. Late at night, DJ Battle called Michelle up to the DJ booth, and she let loose by playing some tunes.

It was a great night, and the next morning we were in our suite at the Fairmont Hotel when Michelle called to me. She had ESPN on, and there on the screen was footage of me and her dancing at our wedding to Montell Jordan's *"This Is How We Do It." Wait, what the…?* Turned out, one of my teammates, linebacker Ola Adeniyi, had videoed us and posted a clip to Instagram. Later, he was real sorry—"I saw other people with their phones out, though," he said.

"Yeah, but they didn't post to Instagram," I said, but I was just giving him shit. It was all good: we were all celebrating, and he just got carried away.

But that video quickly went viral. And I was glad that it did, because the response from the fans made it feel like we had just extended a wedding invitation to all of Steelers Nation. Ola had done us a favor. Seventeen months ago, after all, I'd been carted off the field. Now there I was, dancing at my own wedding. It was the ultimate first down, for them and for all of us.

CHAPTER TEN

THOSE WHO REMAIN BECOME CHAMPIONS

For ten minutes a day, I was back on the field, gliding toward ball carriers, lowering my shoulder into them, hearing the *thwack* of body on body, putting them down. Or I was in the secondary, cutting off a passing angle, picking off a throw, the crowd roaring. Or I was bearing down on the quarterback, feeling his panic as I closed the distance between us, wrapping him up in an angry bear hug.

As 2019 wore on, as my physical workouts made the shift from recovering from paralysis to recapturing football movements, these types of *mental* workouts brought me back into the game. Like a lot of superachievers, athletes have long used visualization techniques as a way to practice peak performance. Now, this shouldn't be confused with wishfully thinking of a better future or with the idea expressed in simple self-help slogans like "See it and you will believe it." No, visualization is, as the saying goes, "daydreaming with a purpose."

NBA great Jerry West was once asked how he so coolly hit so many game-winning shots at the buzzer, which had earned him the nickname "Mr. Clutch." He replied that he'd already made those shots countless times in his own mind. Ever since, before a game, you can find athletes in pro locker rooms sitting still with their eyes closed, rehearsing in their mind's eye the movements they're about to act out on the playing field.

Turns out, there's scientific proof that such visualization positively impacts performance. Studies of the brain show that its neurons, which transmit information, make no distinction between images and real-life action. So when we visualize an act, the brain shoots off an impulse to our neurons to "perform" the movement. This creates a new neural pathway—clusters of brain cells that form learned behaviors and create memories. That new pathway signals our body to act out and commit to memory what we've imagined—even though we haven't actually performed the physical act.

Remember all those hours I'd spend training my turnover muscle memory? Well, you can work on all types of muscle memory without so much as lifting a finger. Studies have been done of NBA players who vastly improved their free-throw percentage without even practicing the free throws. All they did was imagine—in minute detail—shooting free throws, over and over. Until the act was second nature.

It may be an urban myth, but the best-known example of the power of visualization is the widespread story of the prisoner of war in Vietnam who marked his time in captivity by mentally playing eighteen holes of golf every day. He'd walk the course he'd grown up playing, feeling the wind in the air and the sun beating down on him, seeing himself hit ball after ball. When he was finally released and sent back to the States, he made a beeline for that same golf course and promptly shot the best round of his lifetime—without having touched a club in years.

Now, if that sounds crazy, all I can say is call Michael Phelps and LeBron James crazy, because they also swear by visualization. At the elite level of sports, you're always looking for an edge. And when I heard you could practice your craft while doing nothing but sitting still with your eyes closed for ten minutes a day, just like those guys, I was down with it.

For the first six months after my injury, my visualizations were of walking again. But now, less than two years since being injured, I was seeing myself suited up and making tackles. I'd picture every slightest detail: The dirt stains on my uniform. The chorus of grunts and curses on any given play. The feeling of making a hit, as pure an adrenaline rush as I'd ever known.

Meantime, Jerome shifted our *physical* workouts to focus more intensely on football movements. There were backpedaling drills to the point of exhaustion. Side-to-side shuffles. Weight lifting and an intense core regimen. Slowly but surely, I became able to take on tackling dummies, and I was practicing sidestepping or bouncing off blocks. As for running, I started with some light jogging, then gradually turned it up. Eventually I could sprint for twenty yards, at a much slower speed than in my mind's eye, before that damned hitch on my left side would kick in.

Still, I was soon sprinting, pushing, jumping, squatting, pulling, rowing, and lunging every day. When Jerome would bark out an order to do ten reps, I'd do fifteen. When Jerome would whistle the workout over, I'd stick around for an extra sprint or two, or do some more stretching.

In late August 2019, I took to the field before a preseason game at Heinz Field against the Tennessee Titans. During the pregame warm-up, someone caught cell phone footage of me catching footballs one-handed around the twenty-five-yard line. I thought nothing of it, but within a matter of hours the footage had spread across the internet. It wasn't even twenty months after my injury, and there I was back on a football field, nonchalantly catching balls like Odell.

I was surprised by the outpouring this caused—and the speculation. "Pittsburgh Steelers linebacker Ryan Shazier is getting back to business nearly two years after suffering a severe spine injury," said an article on People.com.

"Shazier has already been declared out for the season," wrote the *Hartford Courant*. "But at this point, his goals of playing football once again and eventually becoming a Hall of Famer don't seem all that far-fetched."

I was just doing what I did every day in my workouts. But those who hadn't been tracking my progress were seeing a sign that I just might beat the odds and return to the NFL.

Hearing that speculation was exciting but also worrisome, because, as much as I was practicing visualization, I was also aware of its potential consequences. The Stoics, for example, believed in *negative* visualization. "Who then is invincible?" wrote Epictetus. "The one who cannot be upset by anything outside their reasoned choice."

The great minds, he was saying, don't sit around and fantasize about everything working out according to plan. Instead, they develop the skill to handle whatever obstacle is thrown in their way. They visualize failure in order to prepare for overcoming it.

Now that I was walking, running, and catching footballs on a pro football field, I can't tell you how many times I was asked when I'd be coming back to play. All those questions—from fans, media, even family—were well meaning.

But they missed the point. I had to *resist* focusing on

outcome. In a corner of the San Antonio Spurs locker room is a framed quote from the social reformer Jacob Riis. "When nothing seems to help," it reads, "I go back and look at the stonecutter hammering away at his rock perhaps a hundred times without as much as a crack showing in it. Yet at the hundred and first blow it will split in two, and I know it was not that blow that did it—but all that had gone before."

I'd have loved that even if Michelle *hadn't* turned me into a stone-cold Spurs fan. To give you a sense of just how embedded this philosophy became in the Spurs culture, guess what head coach Gregg Popovich's wine label is called? That's right: Rock and Hammer.

It was a philosophy that bound his team together by celebrating all the hard work the fans didn't see. But for me, it was also a reminder that each rep in the gym—just like every time hammer meets chisel—was an end in itself. That the only thing that's real is *this moment right now*, and to jump ahead to outcome is to actually take a step backward.

It was a fine line I had to balance. At once, I was summoning visions of myself again doing great things on the football field, in order to help reawaken my muscle memory. But if I focused too much on outcome instead of the slow process of making first downs each day, I'd get too far ahead of myself.

No wonder I started to struggle. When my Steelers teammates voted for me to receive the Ed Block

Courage Award, anyone could have sensed my ambivalence. The award is given each year to a Steelers player who had made it back from a season-ending injury. Even though I'd not come back yet, my teammates decided to honor me. And I was humbled that they did. But I was also wrestling with the will-he-or-won't-he comeback narrative.

"To me it's more about showing people that just because things don't go your way you shouldn't give up," I told Steelers.com.

You shouldn't crawl in a shell and lose hope. I go out there every day and do the best that I can to continue to be like I was before I got hurt. If I don't try to get back to where I was, or try to get better, I am going to be stuck in a sunken place. I feel like the only way I can do it is be around the people I love and the things I love doing. It helps me. It's great being an inspiration, but it's tough, too. To everybody else it seems like you are recovering so fast or doing so well. But it's still a battle you have to fight. When you are not on a roller coaster, it seems like a fast ride. When you are dealing with it, it's a lot rockier than you think. Sometimes it's cool to be an inspiration to others so I can uplift people, but sometimes you are still trying to uplift yourself. Sometimes it's hard for me. It's been a long journey. To me, I don't feel like I am a courageous person. Just the fact I am doing this, pushing this one day at a time. I am thankful I am able to show people that just because somebody tells you it's over, it's not over.

Whoa. Reading that now, I can tell I was in a lot of pain. I was wrestling with the expectations of others, trying to remain defiant in my comeback attempt while literally urging myself to take it one day at a time.

As 2019 progressed, I found myself fighting off spells of self-doubt. Sometimes I'd feel utterly exhausted—not by my workouts, but by the enormity of the whole project. It's only natural, right? It's easy to proclaim yourself a man of faith but harder to live true to the old saying, "While we wait, He works."

Thing is, every time I got down, every time I started to think about quitting, every time I began to feel like this journey I'm on was too much for me, literally *every time* I'd get a sign. Now, if you're not a believer, this might sound nutty. But you tell me what Lyon was. How could Lyon's miraculous presence in our lives be anything but a thumbs-up from God?

Or explain this one: During one particularly rough workout with Jerome in late 2019, I had another of those inner self-doubting spells. I'd had enough of all those complete strangers coming up to me on the street and telling me how much I was inspiring them. I'd gone so far as to call my dad and ask him, "What's inspiration?"

I was struggling because my purpose was getting

lost. Was I trying to come back for myself or for others? I *want* to inspire others, but I don't want to *have* to inspire others, you know? I need to do what I do *for* me. Sometimes it feels like a burden to have so many people so invested in what you do. You get afraid of letting them down.

On that particular day, during a hard workout, I was getting exasperated. How many reps had I done in the last two years? Thousands? Millions? I'd gotten better, sure, but was I still progressing? I still had that damn hitch on my left side. While it was not as pronounced as it had been, it was still noticeable. And it was devilish. Because when I ran, I wouldn't feel it for the first twenty yards or so. But as I revved up, it would reappear, as though saying, "Not so fast, homie. You're not all the way back yet."

Jerome knew me so well, he could tell that I was struggling. Normally our workouts are fun. There's a lot of joking, a lot of trash-talking, a lot of laughter. Now I was scowling far more than I was smiling. Jerome knew I tended to keep things in. "Sometimes you need to talk it out, Ryan," he simply said.

"I just don't feel like I have the strength to finish this workout," I said. "It's emotionally draining. I don't understand. I'm not a quitter. But I've been working my butt off and sometimes I don't know who I'm doing all this for."

It was just me and Jerome talking, nobody around us. "I just feel like I need a sign to keep on going," I said.

Just then, Steelers special teams coach Danny Smith came into the gym. We always talked, but this time there were no greetings. Danny just walked past me and said, "Hey, Ryan, those who remain become champions."

What? I'd just been expressing doubt, asking for a sign, and *"Those who remain become champions"* comes flying at me like a blocker on a punt play. I had no idea why Coach Smith said what he said, but it spoke to a place deep in my soul. How is that *not* a sign?

At other times, I'd feel so exhausted—and down—that I'd tell Jerome I wanted to take a day or two off. Well, I'd stay home and play with R.J. and Lyon, and get my *Fortnite* on after they'd gone to bed. And then, when I'd get back to the gym with Jerome, I'd have twice the strength as before. How was that possible? Clearly, my muscles needed some time away to recover. But I also think it was something else, man. I think anytime I'd get too down or close to quitting, He would say, *Oh no you don't. Not when you've got all these millions of folks praying for you.*

Around this time, I called my dad. I told him I'd been frustrated. And he told me that, lately, he'd been watching my highlight tape from my sophomore year in college. "I'm just so proud of you, son," Dad said. "Everything you've been through? You motivate me to keep pushing, to keep going. Ryan, every time I'm feeling down, I put that tape in and you make me keep going."

Whoa, man. Remember, I had asked Dad what "inspiration" was. Well, here he was, showing me: it's a contagion, a two-way street. He was inspiring me by feeling inspired by me. All those strangers who were moved enough to tell me what my struggle meant to them? Man, *they* were inspiring *me*.

Maybe God had nothing to do with opening my eyes to this. But this sort of thing happened too often to be a coincidence. What's that old proverb? "Don't ignore the signs you asked God to show you."

It wasn't easy, but I had to keep reminding myself that when I got down, it was because I had started focusing on outcome—rather than just trusting Him. That's when scripture could bring me back: "'For I know the plans I have for you,' declares the Lord, 'plans to prosper you and not to harm you, plans to give you hope and a future'" (Jeremiah 29:11).

* * *

With my legs strapped in on a leg-extension machine, the docs at UPMC hooked what felt like electric stimulation nodes up to my body. I'd push each leg forward, fighting resistance to extend it, while the jolts of stimulation coursed through me.

What was up with all this?

Well, as best I could understand it, they were testing whether my remaining issues—especially that left-side hitch in my gait—were being caused by muscle or neural deficiency. If the brain wasn't receiving my body's message to move my left side in concert with my right when I walked or ran, there'd be nothing left to do. This would be me. But if it was a muscle deficiency—if, for some reason, my left leg just hadn't responded with the speed and strength of my right—there was at least the possibility of making further progress.

Dr. O was often smiling, but when he brought me these results I could tell he was happier than usual. "Good news," he said. "Neurologically, you're healthy. We don't detect any major deficiencies in your nerves or brain pathways."

"So what does that mean, Doc?"

"Well, it means we focus on that left side," he said. "It seems like you're strong enough, but the question could be one of muscle tone. It may be that it took so long for the left side to catch up to the right that you've developed spasticity in that area."

Spasticity occurs when there's damage to the part of the spinal cord that controls muscle reflexes. That can mess with the signals sent to the muscles, causing spasms, stiffness, fatigue, or, in some cases, a locking in place. At least I now knew that the only thing keeping me from making it all the way back to playing form wasn't a neurological issue. What I didn't know—what nobody knew—was whether my level of spasticity could be somehow reversed.

This should have been good news, right? Yet, now

that we knew that spasticity was the only challenge left to overcome, it suddenly felt like I was face-to-face with that dreaded r-word: *retirement*. I'd been too busy pounding the rock to think too deeply about it, but now that the issue that might keep me from coming back had been *named* out loud, the end felt nearer than it had before. Clearly, retirement had recently been in the back of my mind. Why else enroll in classes at the University of Pittsburgh to complete my undergraduate degree in psychology, with a lot of business courses sprinkled in?

But I'd never really stopped to think about what it would be like to retire in my late twenties—until I learned that it all hinged on reversing the spasticity that I'd developed.

Thankfully, I didn't have time to let my mind race with doubts. I was juggling my workouts, attending practices, and taking a full load of classes. It was a challenging schedule, but, as with so much else in my life now, it felt like I hadn't decided on this route myself. When I'd been at Ohio State a few years before, I'd been more focused and driven than most college students. Most students don't know what their future will hold. They're there to seek knowledge, maybe find some wisdom, and, yes, to party.

Well, my partying days were well behind me, but now I felt like the student I never really got the chance to be. I didn't know it at the time, but I was beginning a search for purpose.

CHAPTER ELEVEN

THE TERROR OF LIVING WITHOUT THE GAME

Behind all the years of practice and all the hours of glory waits the inexorable terror of living without the game," Bill Bradley once said. Think about that. Bill Bradley went to Princeton and was a Rhodes Scholar. After his NBA playing days, he went on to have a long career in the United States Senate. If someone with *that* résumé and background was terrified by the thought of walking away from an athletic career, how hard must it be for the rest of us?

The truth is that there is little in a pro athlete's training that prepares us for transitioning to life after the cheering stops. Many of us have been stars since middle school. In our youth, adults representing high schools and colleges kiss our butts, trying to sell us on playing for them. In our teens, packed stadiums chant our names. The average NFL career is 3.3 years long, which means that most of us are facing retirement in our mid to late twenties—just when the guys we grew up with are starting to settle into adulthood.

"Once you retire, the silence is deafening," John Michels, the former Packers offensive lineman who gave up the game in 1999, told *Sports Illustrated* in a 2014 feature headlined *Life After The Game*. He retired at twenty-six, having undergone—count 'em—six knee surgeries. "No one calls, not even your former teammates. It's like you've been kicked out of the locker room."

Decades after walking away from the game, Michels still had the same recurring dream: he's in the locker room putting on pads and helmet, and as he makes his way to the field, he can hear the roar of the crowd growing louder and louder.

How can you prepare for athletic afterlife? As a professional athlete, we're trained to be selfish. The only thing we're focusing on is the next game. On getting better. On finding a competitive edge. Then we retire—and we're suddenly staring into a professional and personal abyss.

No wonder so few professional athletes reach peace with this most unnatural of retirements. The sports pages are loaded with stories of great stars who couldn't bear retirement and tried to come back for one last hurrah. Whether it's Michael Phelps, Michael Jordan, Brett Favre, or—most notably—Muhammad Ali, few are able to recapture the glory of their youth. In some cases, hanging on too long tarnishes their legacy.

So many try to mount a comeback because athletic retirement is really hard. The statistics are eye-opening: 78 percent of NFL players go bankrupt or experience financial distress within two years of retirement. The same fate awaits 60 percent of NBA players within five years. Divorce rates for retired athletes range upward of 60 percent. The depression rate for retired NFL players is 11 percent, according to a 2006 University of North Carolina study.

I'd long heard the horror stories. NBA veteran Vin Baker, battling alcohol dependency and depression, went through career earnings of some $80 million. Thanks in part to John Lucas, the NBA coach and a counselor to struggling athletes, Baker turned his life around and is now a minister.

Lucas overcame drug and alcohol demons during his own playing days, and he said the deeper issue for athletes who are staring at the end of their playing days is *spiritual* bankruptcy. "The hardest thing is getting guys to see that what you did is not who you are," he said in the *SI* feature.

When former Packers offensive lineman Tom Neville, unemployed and depressed, was shot and killed in a standoff with police three years after his 1995 retirement, his fellow offensive lineman Ken Ruettgers phoned many of their former teammates so they could all talk together, for the first time, about the challenges of transitioning to a normal life after their playing days.

Ruettgers knew that the trauma of brain injury was a growing concern, but he also found that there was widespread depression just from the stress and strain of starting a normal life after a career in the NFL— and he could relate. "I should have been the poster boy for transition," said Ruettgers, who had earned an MBA during his playing days. "But even I was having trouble finding a new purpose, passion and mission. When so much of your self-worth is tied up with what you did, then who are you?"

So Ruettgers wrote a dissertation on the subject of athlete retirement while getting a doctorate in sociology. He also founded Game's Over, a nonprofit that helps athletes navigate the bumpy road of retirement. Today he's a college professor.

The retired tennis great Andre Agassi once observed that "professional sports can keep people from becoming who they really are." That hit home for Ruettgers when his research led him to the Athletic Identity Measurement Scale, a questionnaire that reveals the degree to which athletes view themselves as athletes. He found that we overwhelmingly suffer from "identity foreclosure": we see ourselves as athletes to the exclusion of all other identities, such as parent, spouse, or businessperson.

Former 49ers lineman Randy Cross spent thirteen seasons in the NFL before retiring in 1989 at thirty-four to start a career in broadcasting. He's seen fellow athletes go through what he calls the "separation anxiety" of retirement. "The [media] coverage has exploded since I played, and these kids are having smoke blown up their butts from the early teens on," Cross said. "When that *there's nothing else* moment arrives, they're totally unprepared."

Of course, identity foreclosure isn't unique to athletes. Many highly driven, mission-oriented achievers—think CEOs or politicians—are so successful *because* of such tunnel vision. But most CEOs haven't trained to be a CEO since they were eight years old. They've gone to college and lived a life full of varied interests before zeroing in on their professional obsession. They have a breadth of experience behind them, and losing a job is less likely to trigger a downward psychological spiral. But when an athlete's job is gone, so is the story that the player tells themselves and others about who they are, at their core.

When you're a professional athlete, you're never lonely. You have your immediate family and also the extended family in the locker room. You've got a constant support system—teammates, coaches, trainers—and a daily schedule and routine. It's not just the roar of the crowd that goes missing when retirement hits. It's also the daily structure that comes with being a high-profile athlete.

Nothing illustrates that better than an anecdote once shared by NBA great Charles Barkley. In 1999, he and his good friend Michael Jordan were both thirty-six years old. Barkley's career was coming to a close in Houston—"I'm the artist formerly known as Barkley" he said then—and Jordan had retired from the Chicago Bulls earlier in the year. (A Jordan comeback with the Washington Wizards was still a couple of years away.)

Well, one morning in 1999, Barkley's phone rang. It was Jordan with a question none of us would have predicted. "I just dropped the kids off at school," he said. "I've got nothing to do till I get them at three. What am I supposed to do all day?"

Shortly thereafter, Jordan got hooked on motorcycle thrill racing. Along with his nephew and a group of young adventure seekers, the Greatest of All Time would speed and pop wheelies on deserted Chicago streets at three in the morning. He seemed to be in search of something—anything—that could replace the adrenaline rush of literally being the best in the world at what he'd done for so long.

Of course, you *can't* replace that buzz. But that doesn't mean you can't build a life of purpose and passion after the game, right? To do that, you have to shift your thinking. You have to start preparing for life after the game the same way you once prepped for next Sunday's showdown.

That's what Magic Johnson did, in what still remains the gold standard for transitioning from a sports career. He started thinking about life after basketball while still playing—literally. He'd just watched his Lakers teammate Kareem Abdul-Jabbar encounter financial difficulties. During a home game, he paused while inbounding the ball in front of two courtside season-ticket holders, music executive Joe Smith and Hollywood mogul Peter Guber, and asked them, "How do I get into business?"

Smith and Guber set Johnson up with powerful Hollywood agent Michael Ovitz, but Ovitz blew him off, saying he didn't do business with athletes. "It's the only time in my life I felt five foot nine," Johnson said. Three weeks later, when Ovitz summoned Johnson to a surprise follow-up meeting, Johnson knew that he had to put his ego aside to succeed. In their first meeting, Ovitz handed Johnson a copy of the *Wall Street Journal*. "The thing first you have to do is get your head out of the sports pages," Ovitz said.

Ovitz mentored Johnson and was helpful in setting up Johnson's first business deal—part ownership of a Pepsi bottling plant—which started Johnson on his way to building an empire that empowers Black businesses and employs thousands of Black people.

Like the great point guard he was, Johnson purposely constructed a retirement game plan. Could I do the same? I knew that it would require many of the traits I'd exhibited in my football career: hard work, preparation, and curiosity.

In football and in life, I was naturally curious about what other people did and always eager to learn. Back before my injury, I'd found myself in a luxury box at a Pittsburgh Penguins game, seated near the team's minority owner, Bill Kassling, former chairman and CEO of the Wabtec Corporation, a $1 billion Pittsburgh public company that makes products for locomotives, freight cars, and passenger transit vehicles. After our conversation at the game, Bill invited me to lunch a few times. Each time, I'd show up with a pen and pad, in which I'd furiously scribble notes while he recounted his extraordinary rise in the business world.

At retirement, athletes are still young by society's standards. They're not stepping away from the game to sit in a rocker on a porch somewhere. No, challenges still await, if you're open to them. You have to heed the Stoics and see opportunity in whatever it is that comes next. "I do recommend retirement to you, but only that you may use it for greater and more beautiful activities than those which you have resigned," wrote Seneca.

That requires rethinking your definition of success. For years, success to me meant realizing my dreams: making it to the NFL, making the Pro Bowl, making millions, leading my team to a championship. But maybe a different, deeper type of success was waiting to be discovered.

"At the end of the day, transition is an opportunity to do something for other people," said Ruettgers, who made helping other former jocks part of his life's mission. "That's where real purpose comes from."

Real purpose. My faith tells me that we are right where God wants us to be—we just have to be open to meeting the moment He's given us. "He's preparing you for what He's prepared for you," goes one old saying.

Remember Michels, the former lineman who, fifteen years after retiring, still dreamed of playing? He battled depression—"You have to mourn the loss of your athletic career like it was a loved one," he said—before deciding that what he really wanted to do was help other athletes avoid injuries like his. He didn't have a degree in any of the sciences, but he resolved nonetheless to become a medical doctor. Twelve years and countless student loans later, today he is a surgeon at the forefront of using interventional radiology techniques in orthopedic surgery.

"Medical school was easy compared to training camp," Michels said. "When I perform surgery, I don't have some three-hundred-pounder trying to knock the scalpel out of my hand."

Michels found his purpose and real fulfillment after his playing days by standing for something bigger than himself. By serving others.

"We have the opportunity to use our celebrity to reshape society rather than just entertain it," wrote NBA legend Kareem Abdul-Jabbar in the *Guardian* in an essay with the headline "When Athletes Retire We Face the Most Difficult Question: Who Are We?" "Some may choose politics: the NBA's Kevin Johnson and Dave Bing went on to serve as mayor of Sacramento and Detroit respectively while NFL quarterback Jack Kemp served in the House of Representatives for 17 years....Holding political office isn't the only way to alchemize celebrity into social change: speaking out and lending your name or presence to social causes you believe in doesn't diminish your celebrity, but rather gives it meaning because now your name isn't only related to how well you handled a ball, a bat, or a stick, but how committed you are to a community."

Abdul-Jabbar suggested putting the same passion we'd brought to our game into making the world a better place—in whatever form that might take. "In W. B. Yeats' famous poem '*Sailing to Byzantium*,' he describes aging into uselessness perfectly: 'An aged man is but a paltry thing, / A tattered coat upon a stick...'" wrote Abdul-Jabbar. "But he follows that depressing diagnosis with an inspiring remedy: '...unless / Soul clap its hands and sing...' If we tap into the energy and commitment in our souls, we can invigorate ourselves, inspire others, and improve the world we all live in. Then we are more than great athletes, we are worthy human beings."

Look around: the athletes who have most figured out this retirement thing all seem to have become humble servants of a greater good. Whether it's Agassi's charter school for underserved kids in his hometown of Las Vegas; tennis prodigy–turned–nun Andrea Jaeger's camps for ill, abused, and at-risk kids; Magic

Johnson's inner-city economic empowerment initiatives and his leadership on AIDS issues; Barkley's charitable donations—millions per year—to the Alabama schools of his youth; or the late Nick Buoniconti's tireless efforts to find a cure for spinal cord injuries, the conclusion is undeniable. The ex-jocks who flourish after the cheering dies down all seem to recognize the power of doing God's work in the here and now.

* * *

As 2019 gave way to 2020, it was getting harder and harder to get my butt into the gym. I'd be hanging at home, playing video games with R.J. before looking at my watch: *Oh, snap, I'm gonna be late to meet Jerome.*

Before, hitting the gym had never felt like something I *had* to do. It had always been something I was *meant* to do. Oh, once I was there, I'd go at it full strength. But what did this change say about me and the comeback road I was on? More and more, I was being driven by a sense of obligation. All those fans, my teammates, even the media—I couldn't let them down by giving up, could I?

But luckily, I had the wisdom of the Stoics by my bedside. "What really frightens and dismays us is not external events themselves, but the way in which we think about them," wrote Epictetus. My anxiety over letting people down? That was all me, thinking. One thing I had control over was *that*—my own thoughts.

Besides, if someone felt let down because I never played again, what did that ultimately have to do with me? Hadn't I done my best to come back? "Do you think that anybody can damage your soul?" wrote Epictetus. "Then why are you so embarrassed? I laugh at those who think they can damage me. They do not know who I am, they do not know what I think, they cannot even touch the things which are really mine and with which I live."

The Stoics have this word, *sympatheia*, which refers to the idea that we're all connected and dependent upon one another. "The universe made rational creatures for the sake of each other, with an eye toward mutual benefit based on true value and never for harm," wrote Marcus Aurelius. "You've been made by nature for the purpose of working with others."

The idea is as old as history, right? We all breathe the same air, walk the same earth, love our children. We're all our brothers' keepers. The more I reflected on all those other athletes who had found something bigger in retirement to stand for, the more I kept coming back to this idea of *sympatheia* and to my faith that God had a plan for me.

Early in my rehab, I'd see a fellow patient working out once or twice and then not see them again for a week or two. Meanwhile, I was working out damn near every day. I'd ask the PTs about it: How come other patients weren't putting in the time that I was?

Many insurance plans cap their visits at thirty, I was

told. And often they lacked transportation or caretaker support to get to treatment. That was crazy, I said. Recovering from spinal cord injury requires an urgent, all-hands-on-deck approach, the kind I'd had since day one. How fortunate was I? I had great insurance and money on my own to invest in my recovery. I had access to the best medical professionals. And I had a whole city pulling for me. I can't tell you how many patients I met who had so little by comparison.

On some level, I knew that this was another sign. It wasn't just that I was feeling sluggish about going to the gym—though it was becoming harder and harder to leave the cocoon of my family every morning. But I was also starting to feel called to do something that might just be bigger than football. God's plan might not have been the plan I'd had for myself, but He had put me here for a reason. Seeing all those in rehab who had it so much worse than me set off my own *sympatheia*. By the fall of 2020, I was talking to Dad about just how ready I was to put myself in God's hands and trust His way.

"Son, you're going to inspire more people and help more people than you ever would have winning the Defensive Player of the Year Award," Dad said.

Amen, Pastor, amen.

CHAPTER TWELVE

AH ... PURPOSE!

When I was younger, I was inspired by LaDainian Tomlinson's jukin' and jivin' on the football field. He was a bad man with a ball in his hands, rushing for nearly two thousand yards in 2006 with the San Diego Chargers. I'd watch him and—even though I saw myself as a defensive player—his striving for excellence always gave me something to shoot for. Who else inspired me? I guess my mom and dad, with all their wisdom and tough love through the years.

But that was about it. That's what was so crazy about all those folks telling me how much I inspired them after I got hurt. I couldn't think of that many inspirational heroes in my own life—*until* I got hurt, that is. Then it all became clear. Man, those docs like Dr. O and Dr. Maroon, all those nurses and orderlies, the PTs who coached and drove me every day—they were all real heroes. They were so committed and so selfless that it made me want to go the extra mile for them. I couldn't let them down.

There was also another group of folks who inspired me every day: my fellow patients. TV reporters and print journalists were real interested in how I was doing in the hospital and at rehab, but that was only because, before getting injured, my job had been done in public for so long. I was known. But let me tell you—if you knew the stories of so many of those I met during my time at UPMC, they'd inspire you at least as much as I do.

The more I thought about it, the more unfair it seemed that I'd get all this attention for inspiring others while so many of my fellow patients were inspiring me. That's what first prompted me to reach out to the higher-ups at UPMC with the idea of sharing the spotlight with many of the hospital's everyday heroes who don't get media attention. We decided to produce *50 Phenoms*, a series of video interviews I'd conduct with UPMC patients who inspired me.

I introduced viewers to Joe Aigner, for example. Joe is a healthy-looking middle-aged guy; to look at him, you'd never believe what he's been through. Hospital staffers had a nickname for him: "Miracle Man."

Joe's story started one day when he couldn't swallow a piece of steak. He'd chew, but it just wouldn't go down. Joe's wife, Carol, a registered nurse, insisted he undergo some tests. An endoscopy revealed a tumor.

He had esophageal cancer, which is rare and deadly, with a five-year survival rate under 20 percent. It's especially deadly at later stages, when the cancer advances to other parts of the body like the lungs or the liver.

Joe was at stage IV: scans revealed the tumor had spread to the lymph nodes in his neck. Doctors told him they'd fight like hell for him, but he ought to put his affairs in order just in case.

But Joe had no plans of dying. His daughter, Izabela, was three years old at the time of the diagnosis. "I wasn't going to leave her," he told me.

Because of his swallowing problems, Joe needed a feeding tube. Then came multiple rounds of radiation and chemotherapy. His tumor shrank, but then chemo's side effects started kicking in.

He developed gout, a form of arthritis that causes pain, inflammation, and swelling in joints.

Then came shingles—a painful rash caused by the same virus that causes chickenpox—on his back. "It just starts to get to the point where you have to laugh," Joe told me. "You have to move through it. You just sit there, and you go, 'Well, it's just another day. We've got to just keep moving on.'"

At one point, Joe's weight dropped below one hundred pounds. He couldn't pick up and hold his daughter, an especially difficult blow for him. But he knew he had to keep fighting.

"It was just a day by day," Joe said. "You know, you

just get up every day, and you say to yourself, 'I'm not going to die today.'"

Before surgery to remove the now-shrunken tumor from his neck, Joe took a routine presurgery stress test that revealed four blockages to the arteries supplying blood to his heart. Joe needed heart surgery before doctors could address the tumor in his esophagus.

A month after his coronary bypass surgery, Joe had the esophagectomy. That was a fourteen-hour procedure, and he was in a medically induced coma for two days after the surgery.

The surgery was successful. The tumor was removed. But Joe wasn't done having setbacks.

"My daughter had been waiting patiently for nearly a year for me to be able to pick her up again," Joe told me. "So as soon as I got that okay, she was excited to have me pick her up. I pick her up, and immediately I had this pain in my back. I felt a pop."

Two of Joe's vertebrae in his back had collapsed, yet another side effect of all the chemotherapy and radiation. One more surgical procedure fixed that, finally putting Joe back together again.

Talking to Joe about how he was motivated to be there for Izabela's growing up got me choked up. Can you believe the inner strength of this dude? I felt humbled to be in his presence. I told Joe he really was the "Miracle Man." But he corrected me. The miracle didn't come from him.

"I'm not the 'Miracle Man,'" he said. "I'm a miracle of prayer and modern medicine."

I've walked away from each *50 Phenoms* interview not only moved but a better man. In another episode, I chatted up Brandi Darby, the first blind athlete to place in a USA Weightlifting–sanctioned competition. Brandi was born with albinism, a condition that can affect the pigment in the skin, hair, and eyes. When she was born, her eyes were misshapen and underdeveloped, leaving her legally blind. She has astigmatism, which makes things appear blurry, and nystagmus, which causes involuntary eye movements that can create problems with depth perception, balance, and coordination.

Brandi and I bonded over growing up with conditions that made us appear different from other kids. She'd put up with the same type of teasing and bullying that I'd endured. And she'd found an outlet in weight lifting. "I just wanted a place to put my aggression," she told me.

I could totally relate to Brandi's drive and spirit. When she tore not one but two medial collateral ligaments (MCLs) in her knees, her focus was on coming back. "You know, when you have caretakers and professionals and they're like, 'We can get you out of pain,' and you're like, 'That's the minimum,'" she said. "One of them was like, 'We might be even able to get you back in heels—'"

"We're not worried about heels," I said.

"Right," Brandi said. "I'm like, 'Can I squat?'"

Brandi talked about how depressed she got after her knee injuries. She was being told that her career was likely over, but she wasn't about to give up. "You having albinism and being legally blind, in your mind, are you, like, 'This isn't the toughest thing I ever dealt with before'?" I asked.

"It's true and it's kinda ironic, right?" Brandi said. "Because it turns into an advantage that you have over people who haven't had to face as much. It can be true that I have a disability, it can be true that I'm Black, it can be true I'm a woman, it can be true that all those things at times are disadvantageous, but those things don't have to define me. I can make advantages out of each and every one of those identities, as well."

Listening to Brandi made me want to go straight to the gym. That defiance, that will. We talk in sports all the time about showing what you're made of. What Brandi showed? That's called *character*.

In another episode, I sat down with my Steelers teammate, running back James Conner. James was a rookie on the 2017 team—my last season—after beating Hodgkin's lymphoma. He's written a book—*Fear Is a Choice*—and his story of resilience has impacted many in the cancer community. We compared notes on facing adversity and how, through our challenges, we've both discovered the importance of faith and humbly serving others.

"God got his hands on everybody, so for him to slow me down and say, 'I want you to deal with this, get through this; I want you to impact these people, spread love, show me how important impacting people is,' that is the only reason I went through what I went through," James said. "To impact those people and make a difference and have it not be about me but be about other people."

One day, the folks at UPMC called to tell me about a special case they thought I'd be interested in. Along with retired marine Brandon Rumbaugh, who'd lost both of his legs in 2012 after stepping on an IED in Afghanistan, I went to UPMC Mercy to visit Kristin Fox, an assistant principal from Ohio with two young children.

She'd had the flu, which had quickly descended into bacterial pneumonia in both lungs, kidney failure, and sepsis, a life-threatening condition caused by her body's reaction to the infection. Kim was placed in a medically induced coma. When she woke up, she discovered that her arms and legs had been amputated in order to save her life. We huddled with her in an emotional visit.

"It takes a village to raise a kid, and it's also the same thing for some of the adversity we've gone through," I told her. "Lean on your family and your friends, just like I have."

She was full of spirit and fight and hope. We embraced and vowed to keep in touch. On my way out of the hospital, I felt a lump in my throat. *This*, I remember thinking, *is what I'm meant to do.* God puts you here, and then it's your job to find your purpose.

Kristin started making unbelievable progress. Initially I visited in order to inspire *her*, but the reports that were coming back during her rehab were inspirational to *me*. Talk about the grind of rehab—Kristin's made mine look easy. She had to learn how to function with two prosthetic arms *and* legs. I just had to feature her in one of the *50 Phenoms* episodes.

"My kids are only seven and nine," Kristin told me. "To have their mom at all was better than to grieve her death....I don't take no for an answer, and I told God I wasn't ready for Him."

"Somebody that's dealing with adversity," I said, "what would your advice be to them?"

Kristin paused and then put into words one of the key takeaways for me from the previous four years. "I have moments of frustration, but I always say they're moments," she said. "I never have a bad day. I make it a bad moment, and then I get over it."

* * *

There are many great nonprofits doing God's work when it comes to fighting spinal cord injuries. I've touched on a few, like Nick Buoniconti's Miami Project to Cure Paralysis, the Christopher and Dana Reeve Foundation, and the Adam Taliaferro

Foundation. But there are many others on the front lines of the spinal cord injury fight. Some strive for a cure. Others help patients adjust to their new lives, providing scholarships, at-home care, and life skills. Still others focus on giving those who suddenly find themselves using a wheelchair something to say yes to, like the Pittsburgh Steelwheelers, which offers coed wheelchair basketball, rugby, and track events.

All do amazing work. In the fall of 2020, I *knew* what my purpose was going to be now. The more I trained, the more I couldn't stop thinking about all those fellow patients I didn't see nearly as often at rehab. They were no different from me. They wanted to get well just as badly as I did. They just didn't have access to the same resources as I had. This systemic inequity simply wasn't fair.

The first eighteen to twenty-four months after a spinal cord injury are the most critical. Your progress over that period of time will pretty much dictate how your life is going to go from then on. Well, I took part in 130 official rehab sessions during that time—and that doesn't even count all the extra sessions I'd do each day with my man Jerome.

But most spinal cord injury patients only receive about thirty rehab sessions before insurance plan limits kick in. I don't care how badly you want to get better—if you're only getting rehab around once a month, the system is letting you down. On average, survivors of spinal cord injury spend fifteen days in the hospital and forty-four days in rehabilitation, and those numbers have been on a downward trajectory for some time. Forty years ago, for example, the average hospital stay was twenty-four days with ninety-eight days of rehab.

About 52 percent of spinal cord injury survivors are covered by private health insurance—but most of them quickly find out just how riddled their insurance plans are with limits that hold them back from recovery. Meanwhile, the costs quickly pile up: trauma care, surgery, rehabilitation (which includes physical as well as occupational therapy and could include speech therapy and mental health counseling), long-term home care, at-home medical equipment like wheelchairs, medications. The first year after a spinal cord injury might cost around $1 million, according to the Reeve Foundation.

Most of the folks I worked out next to at Mercy were playing in a rigged game, and they didn't even know it. As my recovery went on, I couldn't shake the thought of this inequity. Every morning, when I'd walk into our kitchen and hug and squeeze Lyon and R.J., I'd feel incredibly blessed. But it became impossible to fully enjoy those moments knowing that so many who were going through similar struggles hadn't been so fortunate.

And that wasn't just a matter of luck. Obviously, not everyone who gets hurt is going to get better.

But everyone should have the same *opportunity* to get better—and that wasn't happening. We're all in this life together, I told Michelle, and everyone who has a spinal cord injury is now my teammate.

Michelle felt just as strongly about caretakers. When I got hurt, Michelle spent every night by my hospital bed, and my dad took over a month off from work. Not everyone has the wherewithal to make that kind of commitment. We wanted to help families put their best foot forward in what was sure to be the fight of their lives.

So the seeds of the Ryan Shazier Fund for Spinal Rehabilitation were planted. We'd start a nonprofit to give those with spinal cord injuries and their caregivers the support, resources, and funding they needed to live independent and meaningful lives. We'd have a narrow focus. Later on, maybe we'd branch out into advocacy work. But for now, I wanted to get as much help to as many patients as possible who were going through the stresses and strains of rehabilitation.

Time was of the essence. About 294,000 people in the United States are living with spinal cord injuries, and 18,000 new cases occur each year. Most spinal cord injuries—nearly 40 percent—are sustained in automobile accidents. About 8 percent occur during sporting activities. We decided to begin by providing grants, stipends, and support to patients in these two categories, as well as to their families and caregivers.

Now that we had our mission, it was time to do

my best Kevin Colbert impression and play general manager. I knew that our success or failure, just like on the field, was ultimately going to depend on the quality of the team we put together. So we decided to field an all-star team.

Many athletes have foundations nowadays. Often they're run by a relative and lend the athlete's name to worthy charitable causes. I wanted to be more involved. I wanted our foundation to be professionally run, as efficient and mission driven as any successful business. I didn't just want to do some good deeds; I wanted to change the lives of countless people who were dealing with spinal cord injuries. While we'd start out focusing on serving western Pennsylvania, I wanted to grow throughout the country. Why not be the best, right?

Like a GM before the draft, I knew the first step was to put together a roster of the best and brightest. To chair our board, I went to none other than Bill Kassling, the minority Penguins owner and former chairman and CEO of the Wabtec Corporation, who had been tutoring me in all things business.

I first met Bill one day at a Penguins hockey game. The Steelers had just played the Kansas City Chiefs, and I'd had a key pick in that game. I was sitting in the front row at the Penguins game, and fans kept coming up to me throughout the game. I always love interacting with fans, but Penguins president and CEO David Morehouse must have felt I needed a breather, because he came over and invited me to a luxury suite. That's where I met Bill, and from then on, over lunches, I'd pepper him with questions and write down his keys to success in a notebook I carried with me everywhere I went.

In those pages, I'd memorialize wisdom, tips, and anecdotes that came my way every day. In conversations, I'd ask people—whether an NFL star or a high-powered business executive—how they got where they were, and I'd scribble down their answers.

One time, early in my career, I told Coach Tomlin that Hall of Fame linebacker Derrick Brooks was one of my all-time favorite players. Wouldn't you know it, Coach produced the *actual* Derrick Brooks to mentor me, and I filled up pages with his wisdom, like when he told me, "It's not about making *big* plays; it's about playing *every* play." To hear that from a Hall of Famer was like being entrusted with a type of holy grail.

So it was with Bill. He was a Big Ten guy—he'd gone to Purdue—so we hit it off on that front. He'd gone on to earn an MBA from the University of Chicago, serve as an officer in the navy, and then climb the ranks at American Standard before serving as chairman and CEO at Wabtec.

Bill was a very smart, business-minded guy, but he never thought he'd become a big-time executive. He was too busy pounding that rock. I'd quiz him on his leadership techniques and on how he rose to the C-suite. He worked all the time, he told me, but he religiously carved out time to read. You don't want to sacrifice curiosity by being *too* focused on your job. And networking was always key. Business is about building relationships. Talking to folks at a cocktail party may not *look* like work, but it can often be the difference between success and failure.

When I called Bill to see if he'd chair my foundation, he was a yes before I could even get the ask out of my mouth. I told him that I wanted a board that was highly connected and powerful, and—critically—that knew me and knew my story. We'd be on a mission, and I wanted to be in this fight with fellow warriors.

Together, we started recruiting our dream team. Kate Dewey, a nonprofit expert and senior adviser at the prominent law firm of Dentons Cohen & Grigsby, agreed to serve on the board as secretary. My dad was an easy sell on a board seat, as were Coach Tomlin and Dr. O. I was beyond honored when Art Rooney II said to count him in, too.

Another Steeler icon—former safety Will Allen— agreed to join our team. Will had been like a big brother to me early in my career, and I'd learned a ton about how an athlete can thrive after his playing days by watching Will, who'd retired after the 2015 season.

Like me, Will had gone to Ohio State and then made Pittsburgh his home after a stellar playing career. His was one of those post-playing success stories I used to inform my own path. Will had become a successful investor in real estate, technology, and energy businesses; his portfolio included HiberSense, Inc., a Pittsburgh climate-control technology firm, and LUNA Energy Partners, an LED lighting company.

But he'd also made a difference civically. The Will Allen Foundation leveled the playing field for a new generation of leaders by supporting efforts that addressed financial insecurity, workforce development, and the education achievement gap.

There are all sorts of diversity, mind you, and I realized we couldn't overload the foundation board with Steelers family members. Cindy Citrone was the founder and CEO of Citrone 33 Foundation, and she and her husband, Rob, were, like Bill, minority owners of the Penguins. Through her philanthropic work, Cindy was also a force in the city's health and education spaces. She was the mother of four children and a cancer survivor, and she was passionate about expanding access to health care.

Keeping the sports diversity theme going, Penguins president and CEO David Morehouse joined the team as well. Talk about winners: during his tenure, the Pens have won three Stanley Cups.

Daryl Crone was the super-sharp executive vice president of Tulco Holdings, the early-stage venture capital firm started by my man Thomas Tull, the Steelers minority owner—and the dude who had turned me on to Stoicism.

Last but not least, Joshua Pollard agreed to join the

cause. He was the young African American founder and CEO of Omicelo, a mission-driven real estate investment firm with a very simple but bold value proposition: that socially conscious affordable-housing development could help neighborhoods improve, retain their residents, and *still* produce attractive returns for investors. Joshua had also founded a nonprofit, Omicelo Cares, that focused on business and real estate education for students and adults in the same underserved communities where he built affordable housing.

How's all that for a starting lineup? Our first drive together was hiring a CEO, and we scored a touchdown. We landed Caroline Boyce, who had thirty years' experience running nonprofits that made a civic difference, like the Cliveden of the National Trust, the Maternity Care Coalition, and the Pennsylvania Coalition Against Domestic Violence. She had moved to Pittsburgh from London, England, when she was six years old, and she'd been a yinzer ever since. She was more than qualified, but I'm not going to lie: it helped that she was a lifelong Steelers fan.

When we announced the formation of the foundation in late 2020, we raised $500,000 in short order, with an initial fundraising goal of $2.5 million. You know how I'd work out at 4:45 a.m. so I could watch film at 6 a.m.? You know how I'd live, eat, and breathe all things football?

Well, that's how Team Shazier would now approach

making easier the lives of those afflicted with spinal cord injuries. We had a game plan, an all-star team, and a champion's drive to succeed. Spinal cord injuries weren't going away. But we could at least say five simple words to many of those who had sustained such an injury, who were no doubt experiencing all the stress and loneliness and fear I came to know so well:

Help is on the way.

CHAPTER THIRTEEN

"YOU CAN RETIRE FROM THE GAME OF FOOTBALL, BUT YOU'RE NEVER GOING TO RETIRE FROM BEING A PITTSBURGH STEELER"

Right around the time the pandemic hit in February 2020, the Steelers placed me on something called the reserve/retired list, keeping a place for me in the organization but ensuring that my $8 million salary wouldn't count against the cap. Soon after, Michelle and I and the kids all went to San Antonio to quarantine with her family for a month.

One night while we were there, I had a dream. In it, I was playing football again—buzzing across the field, hitting guys, getting hit, feeling free, basking in the cheers from the crowd and the high fives from my teammates. Man, I was soaring. But then, suddenly, it all stopped and there I was, on the ground. Hurt again. Writhing in pain. Darkness and silence all around me.

I shot up out of that sleep, my heart pounding,

brow sweating. At first I was hyperventilating, and then the floodgates opened. From somewhere down deep, I just started to bawl. I hadn't cried like that since I was a little kid—the kind of cry where you're gasping to catch your breath. In the past three years I'd become good at hiding my emotions, the better to keep friends, family, and fans from seeing anything but my brightest face. But now I was sobbing, my face buried in my pillow to muffle my guttural moans. Michelle, alarmed, tried to soothe me with loving pats to the head and shoulders.

"Why'd this happen to me?!" I cried over and over, feeling the frustration wash over me. *Why, why, why?*

I cried until I was spent. And then...I just felt finally empty. The dream, and my emotional reaction to it? I realized what it was: a goodbye. Football was my first love, and even though I hadn't played in nearly three years, we hadn't yet emotionally broken up. Intellectually I knew that you could love something and walk away from it. But I'd been so focused on my task at hand—pounding that rock—that I'd kept the emotions around our pending divorce buried for so long.

I got up. Went into the kitchen. Had some coffee. Soon, I felt calmer and more peaceful than I had in ages. I practically floated back into the guest bedroom, where Michelle was sitting on our bed, no doubt stunned by the emotional display she'd just seen.

I sat on the edge of the bed. "I think my time is up," I told her. Hearing myself say that, I felt something lift from my shoulders. All that pressure. That burden I'd saddled myself with.

"Are you sure?" Michelle asked.

There was no doubt. I felt lighter, freer. It was as if, with that one dream, my subconscious had shaken me awake: *It's time.* I thought of the Stoics, who had preached about controlling what you can control and letting go of all the rest. "I did everything I could," I told her. "I have no regrets."

Within days, I was filled with excitement. I started feeling...*liberated.* I'd spent my whole life thinking about nothing but football. I'd always deeply loved the game, and I always would. But now, at twenty-eight years old, I had no clue whether there was something else I could excel at. Wouldn't it be cool to look at that? Even though I'd majored in psychology, I'd loaded up on business courses, too, and they'd piqued my interest in entrepreneurship and real estate.

I was full of ideas, many of which had to do with my desire to help people who were going through what I'd gone through. As usual, Dad had put it all in perfect perspective when I'd first talked to him about the mission of the foundation.

"It's like you have turkey, ham, and all your favorite desserts on your plate," Dad said, "and you look over and someone is sitting there with crumbs on their plate. Now their fight is our fight, son. We gotta make sure they're fed, just like so many other people made sure you were fed."

Still, I knew that my football dream was also my dad's. Telling him it was over was going to be hard. "I've worked my butt off, Dad," I told him. "But I have not been able to get back to one hundred percent."

I also told him that we wanted to come to his house to make the announcement. This wild ride had started with just me and him and a football. We needed to see through its ending together.

So Dad picked me, Michelle, and the kids up at the airport one day in early September. Back at Mom and Dad's house in Coral Springs, Florida, we hunkered down, unplugged, and bonded for a couple of weeks. Vernon II came over, and we spent time together as a family, playing Jenga or cruising the lake behind Mom and Dad's on a rented boat. At night, Vernon and I would sit in the sticky early-fall heat with Dad on his porch, where he'd always done his best thinking. He'd read scripture and all kinds of philosophy out there, a Cuban cigar always dangling from his lips, a Steelers Terrible Towel hanging from the awning above his desk.

Phone calls went back and forth with the Steelers. I would videotape a farewell retirement speech I'd written, and the Steelers would release the video to the media. The team was also sending a tech crew to the house to air a retirement press conference.

Before all of that, Dad called me onto the porch

at about 1 a.m. the night before the tech crew was to arrive. "I need to know where you are with your decision," he said. "And your life." He explained to me that he wasn't worried about what lay ahead for me so much as about my *mindset*. "You're twenty-eight, son," he said. "I don't want you stuck mentally, thinking your best days are behind you."

I told him about all the work I'd done leading up to this moment. How I'd studied up on the pitfalls of athlete retirement. How I was ready for it. How, after that terrible dream in San Antonio, I'd said an emotional goodbye to the game we both loved so much. How the Stoics had convinced me that I'd done everything I could. You control what you can control, and then you move on. "I'm all right, Dad," I assured him, and he seemed relieved.

To officially say goodbye to the game, I wore a plain black T-shirt and took a seat on Dad's porch, the lake shimmering behind me. I stared into the computer screen and started reading the words I'd spent the last few days writing down:

Football gave me everything I could have ever wanted and more. It taught me about hard work, dedication, teamwork. It took me to college and the NFL. It made me money and gave me a life that most people can only dream about. I am here today to make sure the world knows how much I still love football, how grateful I am for everything football gave me, and I am here to let the world know that today I am officially retiring from the game I love so much.

Here I had to pause to fight the tears. Just off camera, there was Dad with tears streaming down his cheeks. I knew he'd cried during the last three years, but he'd never let me see it. Until now.

It has been over one thousand days since I got hurt on the field. To lose the game in a way I had never envisioned has not been easy. When you play the game the way I did, you convince yourself that you are Superman, that nothing can stop you. But then, the moment I got hurt, I stopped being Superman, and that was difficult to make sense. But the way I look at it, God put us all here for a purpose. For twenty years, he let me play football, and now it's time for me to do what He wants me to do. I am going to step away from the game for a while and see what else life has to offer. I know football will always be here for me if I need it, but right now I am excited to explore some new challenges and different paths.

In thanking the Steelers, I revisited one of those early days in my rehab when Coach Tomlin and Kevin Colbert came to the gym to see how I was coming along:

I had a long way to go, but I remember looking over and seeing them watching me as if they were at a pro day or a combine. Right then, I knew I never had a doubt how much they cared about me as a person and not just as a player.

Finally, I had to shout out the Burgh:

You have been with me ever since I was drafted, through good times and rough times, but never more than during my recovery. Thank you to every Pittsburgher for your support, and thank you to everyone over the country and all around the world who prayed for me. I needed your strength and your spirit, and you gave it to me.

The Zoom press conference was also an emotional roller coaster. I began by thanking the media in attendance for "allowing me to tell my story at my pace." And I singled out Dr. O, Dr. Maroon, UPMC, and the University of Cincinnati Medical Center for all they'd done for me. "This is a little bittersweet," I said. "Because I never expected it to end so soon. I didn't think I'd be saying I'd retire at twenty-eight years old, but at the end of the day God has a plan for us, and I'm excited for what's next."

Then a couple of surprise visitors popped up on the screen and my eyes widened: it was Coach Tomlin and my man Vince Williams.

"When I think about you and your growth and development, I think about you two [Vince and me] and I think about the mornings where you two guys really sharpened your sword and developed your love for the game but [also], more important than that, your commitment to the game," Coach said. "I'd grab a cup of coffee, man, and come in there and watch you guys grow with the game of football. Man, more than anything I just want you to know how fun it was for me to watch that natural development. I appreciate you for allowing me to be a part of that. I got nothing but love for you, man, and this is just the beginning, man, as you transition. We really wanted to be here to let you know we love you, brother, and we are really looking forward to watching you make the next step in life and being part of that as well and seeing the greatness that God has in store for you as well."

I had a lump in my throat; before I could say anything, Vince jumped in.

"I just want to tell you I love you, man, and thank you for all the memories we have together, man," he said. "I just want to let you know you were always a much better person than you were a football player, and when you're a person like that, that's always going to translate into things off the field. So I'm just so excited to watch you attack everything else like I got to see you attack football, with that lion's aggression, man. I just want to let you know I love you, bro, and I'm excited about what you got going, bro."

When they both exited the screen, there was a pause. I looked up at Michelle, who was tearing up off-screen, in front of me. "Man, that almost made me cry," I said.

Then it was time to take questions from the press. First, I was asked, why make the decision now?

"You know, the last few years I've been working my tail off to come back and play," I said. "Me and my wife talked about it, and I just felt it was time to transition, to focus on my family more and the next steps in my life. You know, it was tough for me. Like many football players, we try and hold on for as long as possible. My rehab is continuing to still get better, but I just feel God has another plan for me....Obviously, I didn't come back and play football again, but I'm still getting better and getting healthier, so I'm completely happy with where I'm at now. At first, it was tough, but right now I'm happy."

A reporter asked about my emotional reaction to hearing what Coach Tomlin, Vince, and other teammates had to say. "It's very touching," I said. "Sometimes it's really hard for me. Everybody I played with, even the younger guys, they all know what I put into the game. They know how much I love the game. To know they supported me and were there for me and still love me in the situation I'm in, it really means a lot. Not everything ends the way you want it to end, but I'm excited about the future."

I talked about what would be next for me, the

foundation, helping others, my interest in business, and keeping my hand in football commentary by doing a weekly podcast. One reporter said that my teammate T.J. Watt had raved about how I'd mentored players since my injury and that he thought I'd make a good coach.

"I'm not ever going to cancel out me returning to the game as a coach," I said. "I started learning about football at five years old and I'm still going to be learning about football. I just love the camaraderie, just being there with your teammates, with the staff. I would never cancel that out."

Someone asked if I "harbor any anger" toward football. I didn't, though it had been tougher for Dad to forgive the game after I got injured. To this day, he still can't bring himself to watch the game that was the source of so much passion and joy for him.

"At the end of the day it was a routine tackle. Everybody on this Zoom call has seen me make that tackle thousands of times," I said. "I don't really have anger for the game of football. I fell in love with football when I was five. Some people fall in love with people—you get mad at them, but you always make up. That's how I feel about football."

I was asked about my studies. I had to keep it real, man. "Yeah, so I actually finished my schoolwork at Pitt," I said, laughing a bit sheepishly, before explaining that my graduation had to be deferred a semester because I got a D in a class.

I was asked what would happen if one of my boys wanted to play football. "I'd never push it on him," I said. "If he came to me and was like 'Dad, I want to learn to play football,' then I'd be like 'Hey, I'll give you all the insights and tools I have for it.' I'm going to let him be the one that says, 'Hey, this is what I want to do.'"

Finally, as the call was winding down, the Steelers had one more surprise guest. General manager Kevin Colbert's voice came on. Remember how I talked about his emotional intelligence? Well, my man's voice was crackling with emotion as he put everything into perspective:

A lot of times when players' careers come to an end, we worry about what that next step is for the players, because a lot of times they don't find their way. The one thing I want to do is thank you for easing our worries from the day you got hurt and looking at you today. Never once did you say "Why me," and that gives us the strength and gives others the strength to know that any challenge you can overcome, and you have overcome. And that gives us great security moving forward, knowing that whatever that next step is you're going to be successful. But I just want you to know, you can retire from the game of football, but you're never going to retire from being a Pittsburgh Steeler. And thank you for sharing your life and your career with us, and all the best to you, Michelle, and the boys.

Kevin's voice caught at the end, and that got to me. I was able to blurt out my thanks before the Zoom call ended. And then the screen went blank in front of me.

I was now a *former* professional football player. Was the road ahead scary? By now, I was fully down with the great Stoic Seneca. "For the only safe harbor in this life's tossing, troubled sea is to refuse to be bothered about what the future will bring and to stand ready and confident, squaring the breast to take without skulking or flinching whatever fortune hurls at us," he wrote.

My job now was to attack the rest of my life as if it were an opposing offense.

LESSONS

*It is impossible for a man to learn what
he thinks he already knows.*

—*Epictetus*

As I write this, I'm six months into retirement. Each day, I reflect on all that I've learned these last nearly four years and all that I hope my sons will take as lessons from our long, strange ride.

R.J. and Lyon are still young, so these last years may have just been a blur to them. But Michelle and I are doing our best to impart our own object lessons to them.

Of course I hope that, as my boys get older, they check out the YouTube clips of me wreaking havoc on the football field. But even more than that, I hope they come to understand that their old man embraced living a life of purpose and passion *after* his playing days.

Often when someone leaves a job, you hear the cliché: they've left to "spend more time with their family." It's seen more as a cover story than an explanation. But I'm here to report just how life-changing spending time with family can be. Mind you, I'm not saying that pro athletes *don't* love their families, but in the NFL, family often comes second—a concession made out of necessity because of the demands and pressures of the job.

It didn't take long after my retirement press conference for me to learn just how much I dig this retirement thing. It's awesome to wake up with nothing to do other than make the day into a shared adventure with the people you love the most. We hang around the house, playing Pop-A-Shot; Michelle has even gotten lucky enough to beat me once or twice. R.J. and I go at it in air hockey—and, in case you're wondering, hell if I'm about to let him win.

This time with them? It's priceless. For twenty years—from the time I was five to twenty-five years old—R.J. and Lyon's dad was always chasing excellence on the field. Everything else was secondary to that pursuit of greatness. Now, a new world has dawned. I'm twenty-eight and for the first time in my life, I'm...*content*. There's no pressure. Just love and fun and laughter every day.

That doesn't mean that we're lacking in ambition. I

have big plans for the foundation and some business investments I'm excited about. And Michelle and I have gotten passionate about real estate. One recent night, we were staying in the city before moving into our new, downsized home. We looked out at the skyline of Pittsburgh, and I asked Michelle what she was interested in buying when we started our real estate empire. She pointed to the second-tallest building in the whole city. Yeah, the Shaziers think big.

Of course, if one thing is certain, it's that dark clouds will appear overhead at some point in our future. But, boy, will we be ready for them. Sure, I'd still like to be playing football, but what I hope R.J. and Lyon take from the ups and downs of my life are lessons in bouncing back. Alopecia? No problem. Scoliosis? Don't sweat it. *Paralysis?* Not even *that* can keep me down.

"What would have become of Hercules, do you think, if there had been no lion, hydra, stag, or boar— and no savage criminals to rid the world of?" asked Epictetus. "What would he have done in the absence of such challenges? Obviously he would have just rolled over in bed and gone back to sleep. So by snoring his life away in luxury and comfort he never would have developed into the mighty Hercules. And even if he had, what good would it have done him? What would have been the use of those arms, that physique, and that noble soul, without crises or conditions to stir him into action?"

Crises? The Shaziers have had our share. Rather than feel sorry for ourselves, we embrace all the challenges thrown our way. Because, as the Stoics would tell you, it's only in times of challenge that you get a chance to show what you're made of. Will you wallow, or will you seize the day and find purpose in how you handle setback?

From the time I lay motionless on that Cincinnati field in December 2017 until I retired, I was responding to the "will you or won't you play again" question in some form or another, from fans on the street to media in the locker room. I totally get why folks asked. But I also know now that it was the wrong question all along.

The right question would have been: *Whatever happens on the field, have you found purpose beyond the game?*

And now I know the answer: a resounding yes.

Purpose in family. Purpose in connection—with fans, with teammates, with coaches, with loved ones. Purpose in serving others.

I used to think that scoreboards revealed winners and losers. But the games were what we did, not who we were. When I think about purpose now, I think of something Joe Aigner, one of those *50 Phenoms*, told me: that, ever since his mind-blowing medical ordeal, he looks at each new day as a blessing. "I'm going to make the best of every day, because you never know what's going to happen tomorrow," he said.

That's how I view each day with Michelle, Lyon, and R.J.: as something to attack, to seize, and to cherish. When you've been told that you only have a 20 percent chance of ever walking again, you literally feel God's presence in every step you take.

It's funny. I used to be obsessed with being strong and fast. Now I am humble and so very grateful every time my foot hits pavement.

ACKNOWLEDGMENTS

My hope is that, in the previous pages, I've expressed my gratitude and love for so many who have been with me on this journey. I wish to underscore here just how much my family has meant to me—Michelle and my parents, of course, but also my extended family and friends, all of whom took it upon themselves at various times over the last four years to never let me stop *shalieving*.

A book might tell one person's story, but I've learned that it has a team behind it, and editor Sean Desmond, an all-pro himself, has fielded an all-star cast around him. I want to thank them and my cowriter, Larry Platt, for bringing my story to life on the page. I am indebted to my whole team at Creative Artists Agency and to literary agents David Larabell and David Black for bringing this project to fruition. Thanks also to Patrick Bilow for researching and fact-checking much of my story.

Finally, as I hope the narrative makes clear, I am deeply indebted to the Pittsburgh Steelers and to all of my teammates through the years. And permit me one more expression of gratitude: I want to thank the NFL and the very game of football itself. You were my first love, and you will always be a part of me.

ABOUT THE AUTHORS

RYAN SHAZIER is a former professional football player who played four seasons in the NFL. A two-time Pro Bowl linebacker for the Pittsburgh Steelers, he retired in 2020. He is the founder of the Ryan Shazier Fund for Spinal Rehabilitation, which is dedicated to optimizing neurological recovery and empowering wellness for those with spinal cord injuries. He lives in Pittsburgh, Pennsylvania, with his wife, Michelle, and sons R.J. and Lyon.

LARRY PLATT is the author of five books and coauthor of the bestselling memoir *Every Day I Fight*, the story of ESPN broadcaster Stuart Scott's epic cancer battle. He's the cofounder of The Philadelphia Citizen, a nonprofit news site, and former editor of *Philadelphia* magazine and the *Philadelphia Daily News*. He can be reached at larryplatt.net